All the Luck

A Guide to Becoming the
Luckiest Person You Know

BETH BRUDER

Best of Luck!
Beth Bruder

BETH BRUDER

To Adam,

For making me feel lucky every single day.

Contents

INTRODUCTION

"Success leaves clues." – Anthony Robbins

Some people seem to have all the luck. Peppered amongst the population of ordinary individuals are a select few who appear able to get whatever they want, whenever they want it. They have the best house, the best spouse, the best kids, the best car, the best job, the best body, and the most money. If there is an award to be won, they will win it, and if there is a prize to be had, they will have it. They look and walk and talk like normal human beings, and yet they seem to have superhuman abilities. They play by different rules. Things always seem to go their way. It can be maddening to have to struggle along in your own life when there are those who appear to effortlessly float along from one success to another. How do they do it? How can anyone be that lucky?

If you're reading this book, it is likely because you want to be that person. You want to have that kind of luck. Well, I'm here to let you in on their secret. You don't have to be born lucky. You can learn to be lucky. And I can teach you. I know I can because I taught myself, and I am now the luckiest person I know.

I wasn't always lucky. To make a long and all-too-common story short, I was an ugly kid. I got picked on a lot. I had really low self-esteem, which I carried with me for years. As an adult, my poor self-image held me back professionally and made having a successful relationship just about impossible. I didn't know how to be the person I wanted to be. I didn't know how to have the life I wanted to have. Perhaps because I didn't know how to get what I wanted, I ended up with a lot of things I didn't want: an unfulfilling career, an unhappy marriage, and an uninspiring life. I tried to convince myself that things were okay, but deep down I knew they weren't. And then two things happened that changed everything. First, my uncle passed away unexpectedly. We were very close and his death was devastating to me. It did, however, have the effect of putting things in perspective, as tragic events often do. It became very clear that life is short and not to be wasted. I knew that I had to do something, I just wasn't sure what. This led to event number two.

There's an old expression that says when the student is ready, the teacher appears. Knowing that I was going through a difficult time, a friend of mine handed me a copy of *Awaken the Giant Within* by Anthony Robbins. I was grasping at straws at this point. I didn't really think that something written by the oft-ridiculed poster boy for self-help was going to make a difference in my life, but I was willing to try anything. Much to my surprise, I loved it. It opened my eyes to the way that things ought to be. It taught me that I was in charge of my life and there were things I could do to make it better. A simple enough concept, but one that had eluded me for a long time. I was helped by self-help. I loved the book so much that I immediately sought others. I read every self-help, social psychology, and behavioral economics book I could get my hands on. Book after book after book, by authors from Deepak Chopra to Malcolm Gladwell, and everyone in between who might have some advice on how I should be living my life. Slowly but surely I became the person I had always wanted to be – happy and confident, pretty and popular. The more I grew as a person, the more good things came into my life. I made the brave decision to leave my husband and found that being on my own wasn't as bad as I'd feared. I made a ton of new friends. I had an active social life. I was promoted at work and gained new responsibilities that made my position much more compelling. I even had men fighting over me – ME, the girl who never had a date in high school. And then I met Adam. Adam is the greatest man I have ever known. Not only is he extremely good-looking, but he is kind and generous, brilliant and funny. I am married to someone who is better than any fantasy I'd ever had of what a husband could be.

Now, I wake up every day and see the bounty around me that is my life. I have everything I could possibly want. I have had luck beyond my wildest dreams, and it keeps on coming. I see so many people who are struggling and unhappy, trapped in unsatisfying jobs or unsatisfying relationships, and what I want to say to them all is, "It doesn't have to be this way!" I want them to be as happy as I am. As Anthony Robbins is fond of saying, "Success leaves clues." What he means is that everyone who has been successful got there somehow. If you follow their example, you can have the same success. Now that I have my own success story, I want to leave clues. This is the story of how I got lucky.

THE NATURE OF LUCK

"I'd rather be lucky than good." – Vernon "Lefty" Gomez

Luck is a funny thing. Most of the time we hardly notice it at all, and yet it has more influence on our life than just about anything. Things happen to us all the time that we couldn't have predicted. Sometimes they're great and provide us with amazing opportunities. Other times they're bad and result in health problems or financial difficulties. You can never know what life will bring. By definition, luck is something totally beyond your control that conspires to bring you either great fortune or adversity. If that's the case, then, how can I promise to make you any luckier than you are today?

Luck means different things to different people. Some people, I've found, don't believe in luck. They think that if they work hard enough and long enough they don't need luck. Others rely almost exclusively on luck, and wait around for the day it comes. The way I see things falls somewhere in between. Whether you like it or not, there is some element of chance inherent in everything you do. You can't control the weather.

You can't control who you're going to see when you walk down the street. You can't control the people around you and what they do. You can't prevent car accidents or freak injuries. And you'll have nothing to do with some of the best things that happen to you. You could win big at the casino or inherit some money from a long-lost relative. A chance meeting could turn into a great job opportunity or a great marriage. It's possible that you could make all wrong choices and still luck out, and it's possible you could make all the right ones and still fail through no fault of your own.

Fortunately, there are also plenty of things in life that you *can* control. You can control what you're wearing. You can control what you say. You can control your own actions. You can control how you think. You can control how much effort you put into what you do. You can decide how to respond when things go wrong. You can decide to make brave choices or never risk anything. You can work towards improving yourself or continue on exactly as you are. And many of those factors can and will determine whether good things will happen to you and if you get what you want out of life.

It all comes down to probability. In everything you attempt, there will be some chance of success and some chance of failure. There will be some factors you can control, and some you can't. All you can do is give yourself the best odds of winning. You're more likely to give a good presentation if you practice it first. You're likely to succeed at a sport if you train regularly. You are more likely to be promoted if you ask for a promotion. And you're more likely to win the lottery if you buy a ticket.

There are also ways to increase the chances that you'll

have a random stroke of good fortune. When good things happen to us that we don't anticipate, we rarely recognize the ways in which we contributed to getting that luck. But people who are consistently lucky have more than just luck going for them. The more people you meet, the more chance you have of coming across someone who can give you the lucky break you've been waiting for. When the people you interact with like you they're more likely to do favors for you or recommend you for jobs. And when you expect good things to come your way, you're more likely to get them.

This book is full of information on how to increase your odds of success and your chances of stumbling upon some good luck. Anyone will tell you that if you flip a coin you have a 50/50 shot of it landing heads-up. But that's only if there is nothing you can do to influence the coin. There are ways to get that coin to land heads-up a lot more than half the time. This is why some people appear to be so much luckier than others. If you believe that everyone has the same odds of success, it would seem unfair for someone to win time after time after time. But luck and success don't work that way. The odds aren't fixed, and you can tilt them in your favor. Read on and learn how to make every day your lucky day.

BETH BRUDER

THE TWELVE TENETS OF GOOD LUCK

"Here you leave today and enter the world of yesterday, tomorrow, and fantasy." – Walt Disney Company

Here I present to you the twelve concepts critical to living the luckiest possible life. In brief, these concepts are:

(1) **Belief.** "I think I can." If you don't believe your desired outcome is possible, why bother trying? You can have anything you want in life, so long as you believe that you can.

(2) **Confidence.** "I am the best." You have to *know* that you are amazing, and attractive, and talented, and lovable. The more highly you value yourself, the more highly others will value you.

(3) **Happiness.** "Life is good." Things will not make you happy, only you can make you happy. And if you are happy, the good things will follow.

(4) **Focus.** "I know what I want." If you want to be lucky, you have to know what kind of luck you're looking for.

(5) **Bravery.** "I go after what I want." Fortune favors the bold. The timid aren't lucky.

(6) **Persistence.** "I keep going after what I want." If you turn back at the first sign of trouble, you'll never get where you want to be.

(7) **Flexibility.** "I can handle anything that comes my way." The route from A to B is rarely a straight line. Sometimes you'll have to take a detour, and sometimes not getting what you want will be the best possible kind of luck.

(8) **Responsibility.** "I am powerful." When you take control of your life, you give yourself the power to make it into whatever you want it to be.

(9) **Awareness.** "I pay attention." Be aware of the impact of your actions. Be aware of the people around you. Listen with more than your ears.

(10) **Serenity.** "I am calm." Anxiety and anger are deterrents to good luck.

(11) **Kindness.** "I am nice." You can catch more flies with honey, and both you and your flies will be happier for it.

(12) **Gratitude.** "Thank you." When you are grateful for what you have, you will always feel lucky.

There is a lot of information packed into this book. So much, in fact, that it may seem overwhelming at first. I recommend taking a slow approach. Focus on one tenet at a time and make your way through at your own pace. You don't have to agree with every idea or follow every piece of advice. Do what feels right to you. But I'd also urge you to challenge yourself. The more you put into this effort, the more you'll get out of it. And, as they say in Suzanne Collins's *Hunger Games*, "May the odds be ever in your favor."

TENET #1: BELIEF

"Those who don't believe in magic will never find it." – Roald Dahl

Belief is the first tenet for a reason: everything begins with belief. There's a famous quote by Henry Ford that says, "Whether you think you can, or whether you think you can't – you're right." If you don't believe that you can do something or have something, you will prove yourself right. You are the one who gets to decide what is possible in your world, and if you don't believe that it's possible, it's not. If you want to be lucky, begin by believing that you are lucky. Believe that amazing things are coming your way. Believe that anything is possible. And you will be right.

There are a lot of practical reasons to have positive expectations, which I'll discuss in the next few sections. Research has demonstrated that the way you think affects what happens to you. But the power of belief doesn't end there. There is something magical about belief. When you really, truly believe that something will happen, it will. It isn't the belief alone that makes it happen, but belief plays a critical part. When you believe, you see things differently. You do things you wouldn't do otherwise. You go places you wouldn't go. You take chances you wouldn't take, and you don't stop until you get what you want. Belief is a force that can drive you towards wherever it is that you want to go. It will be up to you to choose whether you want to harness its power and live the life of your dreams or ignore its importance and stay stuck exactly where you are today. Choose wisely.

The Power of the Placebo

"A placebo works only if the patient believes it's an effective medicine. Within strict limits, hope, it seems, can be transformed into biochemistry." – Carl Sagan, The Demon-Haunted World

One of the most common demonstrations of the power of belief is the placebo effect. I'm sure you've heard of the "placebo effect" before, i.e. the phenomenon whereby you think you're taking a particular kind of medicine (but you're not), and it has the same effect as if you were actually taking it. These days most drugs are tested using "double blind placebo controlled trials," in which half the patients get an inactive drug (the placebo) and the other half get the real thing. The "double blind" part means that neither the doctor nor the patient knows which group they fall into. On average, in most trials, about 30% of study participants experience a placebo response, meaning 30% of those taking the inactive drug experience the same effect the real drug is supposed to have. The effect is inconsistent, but when it occurs it is quite real. Patients don't just think they are better; they really are better.

In his book *The Placebo Response*[1], Dr. Howard Brody outlines research conducted by anthropologist Daniel Moerman back in the 1980s.[2] Moerman, who was interested in studying the placebo effect, gathered thirty-one studies of a drug designed to treat stomach ulcers. In each of these trials, the setup was the same: A patient's ulcer would be observed using a scope inserted into the stomach before the start of the study, and the patient's ulcer was observed again after one month of treatment, either with the real medication or a placebo. The success rate of the drug was quite consistent between studies, and the ulcers of about 70 to 75 percent of patients taking the medication had healed at the end of the month. Among the placebo patients, however, there was no consistency whatsoever. In some trials, only 10 percent of patients improved, and in others up to 90 percent recovered completely. Those who wish to argue that the placebo affect isn't a real phenomenon suggest that those who respond to a placebo are just those who would have recovered naturally anyway. However, as Brody puts it, suggesting that there could be such a wide variation in the natural rate of recovery from stomach ulcers is akin to suggesting that we don't know very much about stomach ulcers. Clearly some other factor is at work here.

Before and since Moreman's study, researchers have been struggling to understand why some patients respond to placebos and others do not. Not everyone experiences the effect, and it's difficult to predict when it will occur. One thing the research has made clear, however, is that the more someone *believes* that the treatment is real, the more likely they are to respond. Injections are more effective than pills. Pills taken four times a day work better than pills taken two times a day. Doctors who are convinced of a treatment's efficacy are more likely to have patients respond. Pills with the colors blue, green or purple make excellent downers, while pills that are colored red, yellow or orange work well as pretend-amphetamines. Perhaps the most profound demonstration of the impact of belief on healing is what happens when patients undergo placebo surgery. Because it is difficult to "test" new surgeries, more often than not physicians try experimental treatments on patients with severe difficulties and conclude that if they get better, the surgery must have worked. There is no control group, so the effect is attributed entirely to the procedure. A famous example of an unintentional placebo surgery was mammary artery ligation.[3] Patients who suffer from coronary artery disease experience an inadequate flow of blood to the heart muscle. Back in the 1940s and 1950s, doctors thought that if they tied off (ligated) the mammary arteries, they would be able to divert more blood to the coronary arteries and so improve a patient's condition. Patients underwent the surgery and most responded quite well; for many months afterwards they experienced a dramatic improvement in their condition. The treatment was thought a success. That is, at least, until some doctors thought to try out a placebo version, whereby they'd cut open the patient's chests but leave the mammary arteries intact. These patients recovered at the same rate as those with the "real" surgery. We like to think our science has improved since the 1950s – and thus the chances of having a sham surgery reduced – but a similar study was done in the 1990s demonstrating that patients with a certain type of arthritis responded just as well to fake arthroscopic knee surgery as those that had the real thing.[4] Patients were so impressed with the results that they recommended the surgery to their friends.

Whether we recognize it or not, it's possible that the medical community relies heavily on the power of the placebo. Brody goes on to make the point that in the days before the advent of modern medicine, nearly all drugs and treatments were placebos. For centuries patients have been responding to treatments that have since been proven ineffective. It makes one wonder why we need the pills and procedures at all. The answer, at least in part, is that we still *believe* that we need them. The placebo effect has its limitations, and no one is suggesting that we abandon medical treatment altogether. The effect does, however, underscore the importance of believing in the treatments we are getting. Science has demonstrated that belief is critical to the healing process. And if belief can heal a stomach ulcer, or treat coronary heart disease, or improve the functioning of our knees, how can we doubt its power to have a profound effect on all areas of our lives?

The Possibility of Belief

"The moment you doubt whether you can fly, you cease for ever to be able to do it." – J.M. Barrie, <u>Peter Pan</u>

Another demonstration of the power of belief is the extent to which it defines what is possible. It may seem farfetched to suggest that what we believe is possible impacts what is, in fact, possible. Something is either possible or it's not, and it doesn't matter what you believe, right? One of the best illustrations of why this is not the case is the story of the four-minute mile. For many years runners tried and failed to break the four-minute barrier. A mythology grew around the achievement, and many at the time believed it was physically impossible. The top mile runner in those days, John Landy, made it his mission to run a sub-four-minute mile, but after two years of hard training, he still couldn't get below four minutes and two seconds. He announced publicly that he felt the achievement was beyond his capabilities. And then one day in 1954 a man by the name of Robert Bannister did the impossible, running the mile in a time of 3 minutes and 59.4 seconds. A miraculous achievement, indeed, but even more miraculous was what happened to John Landy. Forty-six days after Bannister's historic run, Landy ran the mile in 3 minutes and 57.9 seconds – a full four seconds faster than he'd ever run it before. Landy – and the rest of the world – believed it wasn't possible until someone showed them that it was.

Chances are, you're not attempting something that's never been done before. But it is likely that you are going to be doing something that *you've* never done before and that can be just as daunting. Do you think it's possible that you could earn ten million dollars? Let me ask another question. Do you think it's possible for anyone to earn ten million dollars? The answer to the second question is easy. Countless people who have made that kind of money will immediately spring to mind. Athletes. Actors. Entrepreneurs. Writers. Musicians. Real estate moguls. Financiers. It's hardly a question of belief if it can be easily proven. It's been done before and will be done again. So, then, why couldn't it be done by you? I'm sure you could come up with a lot of reasons. (For example, "I'm not starting a career in Major League Baseball anytime soon.") But I'm equally certain that you could find someone who was in your exact same circumstance and did it anyway. All you need is an idea and the belief that you can pull it off.

Maybe money isn't what you want. Maybe it's adventure. Maybe you want to be a ski instructor in Switzerland or give snorkeling tours of the Great Barrier Reef. Has anyone done it before? If so, then you could do it too. Or maybe what you're looking for is love, and you're not sure if you're going to find it. You have to believe that you will, or you're certain not to. That was the trap I fell into. When I was younger, I didn't believe it was possible for me to marry someone I was madly in love with. I didn't think that the really awesome guys would want to get married, or, at least, that they would want to marry me. So I settled for someone I thought was good enough, and by doing so I had fulfilled my own prophecy. I believed that it was my only option, and so I took it. It was only once I believed that something better was out there (and got divorced) that I was able to find it.

Usually people decide what they think is "realistic" before deciding what they believe is possible. What I need for you to do is the opposite: decide what you want, believe you can have it, and then find a way to make it realistic. The only limitations on what you can do and what you can have are the ones you give to yourself. You can have anything you want. The only catch is that you have to want it enough to do whatever it takes to get it – and you won't be willing to do whatever it takes unless you believe it's possible to have.

Expectation and Experience

"We do not see things as they are, we see things as we are." – *Anais Nin*

Do you think that if you tried a new kind of beer or

17

coffee you'd like it the same no matter what it said on the label or what kind of package it came in? Because chances are that you wouldn't. As it turns out, your expectations – your beliefs about what you are about to experience – have a huge impact on what you actually experience.

In his book, *Predictably Irrational*, Dr. Dan Ariely describes a number of studies he has conducted to demonstrate the power of expectations.[5] One interesting experiment involved beer drinkers at MIT. Patrons of a particular pub were offered two small, free samples of beer and were then offered a free glass of whichever beer they preferred. The first beer was a typical choice – they used either Budweiser or Sam Adams. The second was the same beer laced with a "secret ingredient" – two drops of balsamic vinegar for each ounce of beer. When students didn't know what they were drinking, most of them preferred the vinegary variety and chose to keep drinking it. But when students knew ahead of time that there would be vinegar in the beer, they almost never wanted more. The ones who had no reason to think the beer might taste bad liked it, while those who were suspicious of it didn't. The moral of the story, of course, is that if you expect not to like something, chances are you'll prove yourself right.

Another study Ariely and his colleagues conducted involved coffee. For several days, they handed out the free cups of it to students, on the condition that the students would fill out a short survey on how much they liked the coffee, how much they'd be willing to pay for it, and whether MIT should start offering this brand of coffee at their cafeterias. In addition to the coffee, they provided the usual accompaniments (sugar, milk, etc.) as well as some strange condiments, including cloves, cardamom and sweet paprika. Each day they offered the same coffee and the same bizarre condiments, but they periodically changed the containers in which the condiments were held. They started with fancy glass and metal containers, moved on to Styrofoam cups, and then used torn Styrofoam cups. As you might imagine, the better the containers looked, the more the students liked the coffee, the more they would be willing to pay for it, and the more interested they were in having it served in the cafeteria. The students weren't adding any of the bizarre ingredients held in those fancy containers to their coffee, but just seeing them was enough to make their coffee taste better. Fancy containers led students to believe that the coffee was expensive, and everyone knows that expensive coffee tastes better than inexpensive coffee. Or does it?

This might not seem so important when we're talking about beverages, but take a moment to think about how much your experience of everything is affected by your expectations of what that experience will be like. When you expect to like something the odds that you will like it go up dramatically. If you're an optimistic kind of person, you'll enjoy every movie you see more, you'll like everyone you meet more, and you'll have more fun doing anything you do. If you *choose to believe* that you will like what you are about to do, or eat, or see, you are much more likely to like it. You can improve your odds of enjoying your experience – improve your odds of having a *lucky* experience – simply by expecting to have a positive experience. A simple change in your mindset can have a dramatic effect on your world.

Perception is Reality

"The moment you label something you take a step." – Andy Warhol

I love this quote by Andy Warhol because it underscores how much a label changes the way we view a situation. As human beings, we walk around all day trying to make sense of the world around us. We're constantly bombarded with information and we have to quickly decide what to make of it. We use clues from our environments and our past experiences to classify what we're seeing. We put a label on it, and once we do, that label changes the way we see that thing forever after. If X, this label I have attached to something is true, then this quality, Y, associated with this label must be true as well. If the label is correct, everything I experience must fit within the paradigm of this label. It is an extension of the concept addressed in the previous section. Just as if you expect something to taste bad, it will taste bad, if you decide that someone is smart, or stupid, or fun, or rude, you will find yourself interpreting everything they do based on that assumption.

An excellent illustration of the power of a label is Dr. David Rosenhan's classic study published in 1973 entitled "On Being Sane in Insane Places."[6] In it Dr. Rosenhan poses a simple question: are people so distinctly either "sane" or "insane" that one would be able to assess their mental state in any environment, or does the environment play a role in the assessment? In his experiment, he had eight people with no history of mental illness present themselves for treatment at twelve psychiatric hospitals across the United States. Each of these pseudo-patients went to the hospital and claimed that they had been hearing voices. When asked what the voices said, they described the voices as being unclear but appearing to say something like "empty," "hollow," and "thud." Beyond alleging this one false symptom, they behaved as normal and described no further mental health difficulties. Despite the lack of any other symptoms or supporting evidence of disorder, each was admitted to the hospital, in almost every case with a diagnosis of schizophrenia.

Once admitted, each pseudo-patient was responsible for getting themselves out, meaning that they would not be discharged until the powers that be felt they were sane enough to return to society. Once in care, they exhibited no signs of mental illness, and yet it still took an average of nineteen days to be dismissed. None of the pseudo-patients were uncovered as fakes, and they were all discharged with a diagnosis of schizophrenia in remission and a prescription for psychotropic drugs. Even more telling were some of the experiences the pseudo-patients had in the hospitals. Given that they had been labeled schizophrenic, everything they did was interpreted as such. Many of the pseudo-patients took lots of notes, as they were, of course, doing research. Medical charts included comments like, "Patient engaged in writing behavior." Given how little there was to do in the hospital, most of the patients, real and fake, were frequently bored. With little else to look forward to, they'd line up for meals long before mealtime. A psychiatrist described this as "characteristic of the oral-acquisitive nature of the syndrome." One pseudo-patient, who had given a very normal description of his relationships with his parents, wife and children, was interpreted as having "a long history of considerable ambivalence in close relationships, which begins in early childhood." Even among trained professionals, once a label had been assigned, everything a patient did became evidence of their diagnosis.

Another fantastic illustration of the power of the label is the effect draft order has on a player's career in the NBA. On its face, the draft is simply a selection process whereby teams get to pick new players from a pool of young talent. Players are usually about 22 years old, but they can be as young as 19. Scouts have a pretty good idea of who the best players are based on their performance at the high school or college level, but it's still anyone's guess how they'll perform in the NBA. The top picks have shown the most potential but are not guaranteed to be the best players a few years down the road. Therefore, it would stand to reason that a player's draft order shouldn't have any long-term impact on their career. But it turns out that it does.

In their book *Sway*[7], Ori and Rom Brafman describe the work of two economists (Barry Staw and Ha Hoang) who conducted an analysis exploring which factors affected the amount of time on the court given to a player in the NBA.[8] Unsurprisingly, those that scored more got more playing time. Somewhat surprisingly, toughness (rebounds per minute and blocks per minute) and quickness (assists per minute and steals per minute) had little if any impact on playing time. Most surprising, however, was the impact of a player's draft order. Controlling for all other factors, each increment in draft number accounted for 23 minutes of playing time in a given season. That means that if you were drafted 5th overall, you would play 23 more minutes than the guy who was drafted 6th overall, and 115 minutes more than the number 10 pick. And this wasn't just in the first season after the draft – the effect persisted through the players' fifth years, the last year included in the study. Even more tellingly, those players drafted in the second round stayed in the league an average of 3.3 fewer years than the first-round picks. Again, this was *regardless of the quality of their play.* Being labeled a top draft pick makes you look like a better player – even if you're not.

This concept is important because of the labels we so often give to things and people. Your beliefs about other people affect the way you view their behavior. Your beliefs about a situation affect the way you view that situation. Most of the time we don't even know we're doing it, but once we decide someone is mentally ill, or an excellent basketball player, we rarely change our opinion. We use the things they do and say as evidence of the label we've already given them. We tend to focus on the things that fit with the label and conveniently disregard the things that don't.

This concept is also critical when it comes to the labels we give to ourselves. Once you have decided who and what you are, you interpret everything that follows as evidence fitting that diagnosis. Whether you believe you're shy or outgoing, quiet or loud, timid or brave, all of your subsequent behaviors are viewed through that lens. Worse, once you assign yourself a label, you choose to act according to that description. If you have decided that you are shy, it likely means that you avoid situations in which you might have to talk to people you don't know or where you might be embarrassed. The behavior reinforces the label. You avoid social situations because you believe that you are shy, and you use your inexperience with social situations as proof of your shyness. The good news is that once you understand the power that labels have over you, you can develop the tools to change them.

Auto Translate

"You create your own universe as you go along." – Winston Churchill

By now I hope you are convinced that the way you see things matters. I'd like to talk for a moment about the process by which you come to see things the way you do. Some of the examples I gave were pretty self-evident. If I tell you that someone is a good basketball player, you'll probably see them that way, and if I tell you that there is going to be vinegar in your beer, you probably won't like it. But most of the time the judgments you make are much more subtle. Most situations require interpretation. The most relevant example of this was the coffee experiment: no one told the students the coffee was more expensive, but when the condiments were served in nicer jars, they made that assumption. The process begins with baseline beliefs, i.e. "Things that are packaged nicely are more expensive," and, further, "Expensive things are better than things that are less expensive." Then there is a visual cue, i.e. seeing a fancy container. This, in turn, triggers an interpretation: "I will like this coffee." We use our beliefs to translate what we're seeing into something that makes sense to us. The translation process is also automatic; the students weren't thinking to themselves, "Oh, the coffee must be expensive and so I'll probably like it." They just liked the coffee without thinking about why. Most of the time this is a very efficient system. We don't waste time wondering why we like one coffee more than another; we just pick one and go on with our day. The system only becomes problematic when our translations have unintended consequences. As in the coffee example, anything that requires interpretation is prone to error.

We tend to think of ourselves as video cameras, taking in every detail exactly as it happens. But that's not how we operate. Video cameras take an impartial rendering of events. We, however, are interpretation machines, and *biased* interpretation machines at that. If five people see the same event transpire, they will walk away with five very different views of what just happened. Sports are an excellent example of this. I'm a big New York Rangers fan. When referees call penalties against my team, I frequently think they are terrible calls, though I imagine the fans of the opposing team would be inclined to disagree. Sometimes a call is so obviously either good or bad that it's clear to everyone, but most of the time it's not. Most of the time it matters whether you're a Rangers fan or an Islanders fan.

In sports, at least, our biases suit us. I'll see the Rangers in the way that's most advantageous to them. In life, however, our biases don't always work in our favor. People who are prone to anxiety tend to see every situation as potentially dangerous and focus on what might go wrong, rather than see all the potential benefits. People who think life is hard focus on all their difficulties rather than appreciating the things that go well. There is that famous expression, "To a hammer, everything looks like a nail." Consciously or not, we classify everything that happens in our lives to fit our belief system, and our belief system can either help us or hurt us. The Greek philosopher Socrates tells a story that explains how this works. Socrates was standing outside the gates of Athens when he was approached by a man who asked him what living in Athens was like. Socrates replied with a question of his own: "What is it like where you live now?" Terrible, the man says. The people are back-stabbers and thieves, and I would be leaving behind no friends. Socrates replied by saying, "I wouldn't move to Athens then, you'll only find the same kind of people here." Another man approached Socrates and asked him the same question – should he move to Athens? Again, Socrates asked him what the people were like where he lived now. Wonderful, the man said, the best kind of people you'd ever want to know. This time Socrates' reply was, "You'll love Athens. We have the same kind of people here."

If you want to change what you experience, you have to begin by changing the way you *interpret* your experience. Some interpretations are beneficial to you and some are not. Because the way you see things affects what happens to you, some interpretations will make you *luckier* than others. It is a powerful moment when you understand that you can decide how you want to interpret what happens to you. You can choose to see the world as a place where good things are bound to come your way. And then they will.

Belief in Action (The Self-Fulfilling Prophecy)

"If men define situations as real, they are real in their consequences." – The Thomas theorem, formulated in 1928 by W. I. Thomas and D. S. Thomas

All of your beliefs affect you in one way or another, but one belief above all others has the capacity to change the whole course of your life. I've said a few times in this chapter already: if you believe that you are lucky, then you will be lucky. It may sound too good to be true, but it's not. What you believe affects how you behave, and the way you behave affects what happens to you. Your belief that you are lucky will prompt you to act in ways that will yield positive outcomes. I'd like to illustrate how this works by using two fictional women, Lucky and Unlucky. Lucky believes that she is lucky, while Unlucky believes quite the opposite. Let's see how this plays out in their lives:

Lucky goes after what she wants because she believes that she'll get it. She devotes herself to her goal because she believes it will be worth it. She takes big risks, believing that they'll pay off. Even if it doesn't work out right away, she believes that it will eventually, so she keeps trying. She persists until she succeeds, which reaffirms her belief that she is lucky. Meanwhile, Unlucky does not go after what she wants because she does not believe that she'll get it. Even if she does make an attempt, it will be a halfhearted one, which won't get her very far. She'd never take a big risk, knowing that with her luck, it wouldn't turn out well. And at the first sign of trouble, she'll give up. It's all the evidence she needs that she is in fact unlucky and should never have bothered in the first place.

Lucky nearly always enjoys the new things she tries because she believes that she will. She loves every new restaurant, every new movie, every party she attends, and every class she takes. She makes new friends wherever she goes because she always expects to like the people she meets. She has so much fun with her life because she is always experiencing good things. Unlucky, on the other hand, almost never enjoys the new things she tries. To her, new restaurants are a waste of money because she never likes the food. Movies don't entertain her. She never likes the people she meets at parties, so why would she bother going? Classes are always boring, so she may as well stay home. Life is joyless and monotonous. Good things never seem to happen to her.

Lucky even manages to heal quickly when she is ill. She believes fully in the efficacy of her treatments and is back on her feet in no time. When Unlucky is sick, it takes her ages to get better and her treatments never seem to work.

I want for you to understand how different life can be when you expect things to go your way. When you believe you are lucky, you give yourself an opportunity to get lucky. You are willing to bet on yourself because you believe you will win. You are willing to try new things because you believe that you will like them, and, as the research shows, you are far more likely to enjoy them when you expect that you will!

Your beliefs affect the way you behave. Your behaviors then lead to consequences that give you either more reasons to believe, or more reasons to doubt. If your belief is strengthened, you'll be even more compelled to action, and if your belief is weakened, action will become more difficult. This cycle of belief, action, and outcome affect every aspect of your life. Having positive beliefs makes positive things more likely to happen. Having negative beliefs makes negative things more likely to happen. It really can be that simple.

What Do You Believe?

The next step to developing beliefs that can help you become the luckiest possible version of yourself is to understand what your beliefs are right now. If you've had your beliefs on autopilot, like so many other people, you may not even know what beliefs you have that are holding you back. Below you will be asked to think about your beliefs in a few key areas of your life.

Beliefs about the World

"The most important question any human being can ask themselves is, 'Is this a friendly Universe?'" – Albert Einstein

Let's begin with a simple exercise. Fill in the blank: Life is _____ . How you answer this question says a lot about how you see the world. Is life a struggle? Or an adventure? Is life tragic? Or inspiring? Is life hard or easy? Is life dreary and boring or fun and exciting? Is life a punishment or a gift? If your life was a movie, would it be a comedy or a drama? Years ago, before I got lucky, I made the mistake of believing that the movie of my life wasn't going to have a happy ending. I loved romantic comedies, which always end with the harried young woman magically getting everything she wants; I just couldn't see it ever happening for me. *Before* I got any of the luck I wanted, I had to believe my happy ending was coming – and that every happy ending was the beginning of a new story with a happy ending of its own.

Beliefs about People

Let's try another one: People are _____ . Are people generally honest, or are they cheaters? Are people helpful, or are they out to get you? Do you assume you will like a person when you first meet them, or do you assume that you won't? The way you see people affects the way you will treat them, and this will affect the way they behave. If you want to have positive interactions with people, you have to begin by believing they will be positive.

29

Beliefs about What Is Possible
"Reality is negotiable." – Timothy Ferriss, <u>The 4-Hour Workweek</u>

What are your beliefs about what is possible in your life? What limitations have you put on yourself, consciously or not? Do you have to stay at your job? Do you have to stay in your marriage? Do you have to stay in your house? And if so, why? There is nothing in this world that you absolutely have to do. Whatever you are doing, you are choosing to do. You may have good reasons to choose to stay where you are; just be aware that you are making a choice. There is always another option. The obstacles to making a change could be daunting – the financial uncertainty that comes with leaving a job, for instance. But it doesn't mean that it's not possible. Leaving my first marriage was hard. But it was also the best decision I've ever made. When you want something enough, you can make it possible.

Many people have a set idea of what options are available to them, and it's a very limited set. They think being successful means having a spouse, a house, a couple of kids, and a job where they sit behind a desk all day. They believe that anything else would just be a fantasy and they are too grownup and responsible for such a thing. There is a lot of pressure in our society to have a "normal" kind of life, and much of that pressure comes from people who have told themselves year after year that it is the only kind of life they are "allowed" to have. It's perfectly legitimate to want the kind of life I've just described. Plenty of people do and are fantastically happy. But if the kind of life you want lies further afield, you're going to have to be brave enough to go after it. You're going to have to believe it's possible to succeed in life without doing anything that might be described as "normal." You're going to have to give yourself permission to travel the world waiting tables wherever you go, or become a skydiving instructor, or open a bakery, or whatever it is you want to do that you might not believe is possible for you right now. It can take more effort to live an unconventional life, but if it is what you desire, nothing will be more rewarding.

There are also those who are stuck where they are because they believe they always have to follow the rules. Any rule can be broken, and you can't let an artificial restriction stand in your way. I once knew a woman who moved to Boston to be with her boyfriend, only to have the relationship end in a bitter breakup shortly after she arrived. She had no friends in Boston and was desperate to get back to New York. She felt she couldn't, however, because of her job. She had worked for the same company for seven years, and this company had a policy that when you take a new position, you must stay in that position for at least a year before applying for another transfer. Having just been transferred to Boston – and gotten a promotion at that – she felt she needed to say at least a year before moving back. My opinion? Screw the policy. The company obviously valued her as an employee. I'm certain they would rather keep her with the firm than let her go because she wanted to move cities before her year was up. Not to mention the fact that anyone would be sympathetic to her plight. All she needed to do was *ask*. All she needed to do was *believe she had the option*. Happily, she is now back in New York and moving on with her life.

There are an infinite number of options available to you, but you have to be able to see the possibilities before you can grab onto them. What would you do if you could do anything? I'm going to guess that your answer isn't, "Exactly

31

what I'm doing right now." Allow yourself to start dreaming. Get excited about your life again. Never assume something isn't possible without first exploring the possibility.

Beliefs about Work and Money

Do you believe that hard work is the only way to get ahead in life? I'll be honest here. I'm going to say repeatedly over the course of this book that you have to work hard to get what you want. But when I do, I'm talking about a very particular kind of work: smart work. As the adage goes, "Work smart, not hard." I want you to believe that smart work is the only kind you'll ever have to do – and that it's a lot easier than hard work.

It's a very American ethos to take pride in doing lots of hard work. There is nothing wrong with hard work, and some is sure to be required. But there are few things in life I hate more than work for the sake of work. When you have a goal, the object should not be to work as hard as possible in order to achieve that goal; the object should be to achieve the goal while expending the least amount of effort. There is nothing noble about wasted effort. There is nothing to be gained from effort directed at something that won't get you any closer to your goal. It's even possible for your hard work to work against you if you're not working in the right way. There is value in not spending every moment of your life working. There is value in recreation and relaxation. Enjoying your life doesn't make you lazy. And taking breaks isn't just enjoyable – it's beneficial to your work. There is a wealth of new research showing that taking more breaks, such as for daytime naps and workouts, as well as taking more vacations, leads to increased productivity. In

2006, the accounting firm Ernst & Young studied the relationship between employee performance and vacation days.[9] The results demonstrated that the more vacation an employee took, the more highly their supervisors rated them; for each ten hours of vacation, an employee's year-end performance rating went up by 8 percent. It's a myth that the person that works the hardest is the most likely to get ahead. It is the quality of the work and not the amount of time it took to do it that matters.

Another area of belief to examine is your feelings on the relationship between work and money. Many people believe that the amount of money they have is directly related to how much work they do. This is not the case. There are ways to make money by doing minimal work. For example, if you own a business, you can pay others to do the work for you. Or, you could own a business that requires little labor to run. Starting a business needn't take a large investment, and it can free you from the need to sit in an office all day. If you're not looking for a fulfilling career and would rather devote your time to your family, or your hobbies, this should be your goal. *The 4-Hour Workweek* by Timothy Ferriss is an excellent resource for tips on how to make money without having to work all the time.[10] Believe that it's possible to earn a living without working very hard and you will be able to find a way.

Beliefs about Love
"Your task is not to seek for love, but merely to seek and find all the barriers within yourself that you have built against it." – Rumi

Let's try another fill in the blank: Love is_____.
Everywhere. Hard to find. Joyful. Painful. The best thing in the
world. The worst thing in the world. A lot of people have
negative views of romance because of things that have
happened in the past. They think that if they are suspicious of
everyone they date, it will prevent them from getting hurt
again. I've said it before and I'll say it again: your expectations
affect your experience. Let's say that two women meet the
same man. One woman is guarded and cynical about love. The
other woman is optimistic and open to whatever happens.
Which one do you think is more likely to live happily ever after?

Aside from love itself, some people have negative views
of men or women in general. Back in my unlucky days, I thought
that all men were jerks, and that no men, or at least no good
men, were looking to be in a relationship. And guess what I
found? Jerks and commitment-phobes. Because that's what I
was looking for. Some men see women as greedy and selfish. A
friend of mine hates the word "date" because he sees dating as
a means for women to get free dinners and drinks. He's so
afraid of getting scammed that he avoids dating altogether.
Certainly, not every man will be nice, and not every woman will
be honest, but it makes a difference whether you think the nice,
honest ones are in the majority or the minority. Give someone a
chance to be nice and honest before assuming they're not.

Some people also limit their chance at love by believing
that they have a particular "type." They'd only date someone
who went to college, or they'd never date someone who had
kids. You can never know who you're going to fall in love with,
and if you'll only ever date someone who meets the items on
your checklist, it might take a lot longer to find them.

Others feel that they've had their chance at love and it's not coming back around again. They're in love with someone who doesn't love them back, or the person they love left them or cheated on them or passed away. Love isn't a onetime deal. There is no such thing as one perfect person for you. There will be many, many people over the course of your life who it will be possible for you to fall in love with. It may not always feel that way, but it's true. Keep your eyes – and your heart – open.

Beliefs about Health and Age

What are your beliefs about your health? Do you believe it's possible for you to be skinny and fit? Do you believe that you're the kind of person who gets sick all the time? Do you believe you're going to be a healthy and active senior citizen, or you see yourself immobile and in a nursing home?

When it comes to beliefs about your weight many people find it hard to believe that they could ever be thin. In particular, people who have been overweight all their lives have trouble envisioning themselves at a healthy weight. Belief that it's possible is critical to the process. It's also important to examine your beliefs about how difficult it would be to eat healthfully and get enough exercise. Remember again that your expectations affect your experience. If you expect not to like healthy food or if you expect to hate spinning, you probably will. Motivate yourself to have the opposite expectation and see what happens.

When you believe you are sick all the time, it affects what you notice. Remember that beliefs impact the way in which you interpret subjective information. Are you hyperaware of every ache and pain? Do you take note of every cough and sneeze? Do you have a headache and worry that it's a brain tumor? Not only can you convince yourself that you are sick all the time by focusing on minor, everyday symptoms, but you can *make yourself sick*. Stress and anxiety weaken your immune system. Further, recall the section on the placebo effect. If it's possible to take an inactive drug and have your body heal itself, it is equally possible for your body to make itself sick or slow down the healing process. Your body is even capable of counteracting an active treatment. A famous study was conducted by Dr. Henry Beecher at Harvard Medical School with 100 students, in which half of them were given sleeping pills but were told they were amphetamines, and the other half were given amphetamines and were told they were sleeping pills. The drugs didn't have the effect they were designed to have – they had the effect the students *believed* they would have. Many were wide-awake despite just having just taken a sleeping pill, and many were falling asleep despite having just taken an amphetamine. Believe that you are a healthy person and you will be healthier.

What are your beliefs about aging? It matters because if you have negative beliefs about getting older, you might be speeding along the process. In a 2006 study, researchers measured the hearing of 546 adults aged 70 to 96 years old.[11] At the same time, they asked study participants, "When you think of an old person, what are the first five words or phrases that come to mind?" Three years later, the hearing of the same group of adults was measured again. The hearing of most of the group had declined, as one would expect. But the hearing decline was worse for some than others; independent of age and health status, those that experienced the most hearing loss were those that had the most negative views of old age.

36

Researchers estimated the decline among the pessimists in the group was the equivalent of eight years of normal aging. Having positive beliefs about old age can actually keep you young.

A Change of Belief

Perhaps you've now identified a few beliefs you'd like to change. The question becomes how you might go about changing them. For any belief that is holding you back, the following four steps should help you to rid yourself of it:

(1) **<u>Determine where the belief came from.</u>** Everything you believe came from somewhere. Identifying the reasons *why* you believe something can help you to change that belief. Often our dysfunctional beliefs developed in childhood. Some people had parents who made them feel bad about themselves or made them see the world as a place full of scary people and dangerous things. Others were bullied in school and were made to feel unattractive and unworthy. Things that we "learn" when we're young often stick with us even when those "lessons" impact us in a negative way. Dysfunctional beliefs can also be formed after childhood, often as a response to an emotional incident. If a loved one cheats on you it can make you believe that all relationships are bad, or if you are fired from a job, it might make you believe that you're incompetent. What has happened in the past does not have to dictate what happens in the future. A change in belief can lead to a change in outcome.

(2) **Find a replacement belief.** If the original belief is not true, then what is true? It may seem as though the new belief should be the exact opposite of the old one, but that generally isn't the case. If the original belief is "I screw up everything," the replacement belief shouldn't be, "I get everything right." The new belief must be reasonable. It has to be something that you can convince yourself is true. A better option might be, "I give everything my best effort. Sometimes I get it right immediately and sometimes I will need to keep trying." No one gets everything right *all the time*. No one *always* succeeds. No one is *always* lucky. If you need to be good at everything immediately to feel as though you are a success, you are setting yourself up for failure. Anyone would feel like a loser if their definition of a loser is someone who fails at anything at all. Frame your new beliefs in such a way that you give yourself a chance to believe them.

(3) **Find support for the new belief.** As mentioned, dysfunctional beliefs are often formed in childhood or as a consequence of an emotional event. But dysfunctional beliefs are *maintained* through a different mechanism. Our beliefs affect the way we interpret what happens to us, and our beliefs affect what we notice. In order to maintain the old belief, you were likely interpreting situations in such a way that they became evidence for the old belief. Let me refer back to the example of someone who

believes they are always sick. For the sake of illustration, let's assume for the moment that you are one of those people. You would interpret a headache as a sign of a brain tumor. You are also likely to notice every ache and pain and pay close attention to every story in the news about increases in the rate of cancer or heart disease. In order to change your belief, you need to change your interpretations and change what you notice. Instead of a brain tumor, interpret your headache as a sign that you're dehydrated. Notice days when you feel great and take that as evidence of your fantastic health. Pay close attention to stories about miracle recoveries and how exercising can keep you healthy. Train yourself to look for evidence supporting your new belief rather than evidence against it. See an example of something that contradicts your old beliefs and force yourself to focus on it. Remind yourself of this new evidence the next time you come across something that appears to confirm your old belief. Go even further and test your new beliefs. If your old belief was that you are too sick to be a runner, start a running program and see how it goes. When you test a new belief, it's critical to give it a real try. Making one half-hearted attempt doesn't count. You have to try consistently, for a long time, and with real effort, for it to count.

(4) **Reinforce the new belief.** In some ways, this is the hardest part. It's easy to have a new belief when you are calm and well rested and things are going

well. But when something happens to throw you off, you will find it all too easy to fall back into your old pattern of belief. Don't let yourself do it. Step 3 is critical because you must have good supporting evidence for your new belief to turn to in times of doubt. And you must support your new belief over and over again. Changing beliefs requires discipline. Remember that you are in charge. You are in control. And you get to decide what you believe.

Caveat

Keep an Eye Out

While I encourage you to believe everything is going to work out and all things will go your way, it's still vitally important to be aware of any problems that might arise. Believing in a positive outcome isn't an excuse to be unprepared. Cover all your bases and have a backup plan in case things don't go as well as you hope they will. Placing too much stock in your good luck is just as dangerous as placing too little. You can never count on luck alone to get you through.

Belief Alone Is Not Enough

Belief is the first step towards getting everything you want out of life. But it is only the first step. There is a lot more that goes into getting lucky.

TENET #2: CONFIDENCE

"You yourself, as much as anybody in the entire universe, deserve your love and affection." – Buddha

"No matter how good you are, if you're not promoted right you won't be remembered." – Andy Warhol

Confidence, first and foremost, is about loving yourself and believing that you are the most wonderful, attractive, and intelligent person there is. But there's more to it than that. It's also about how you present yourself to the world. When you see yourself in a positive light, you invite others to see you that way as well. When you feel that what you have to offer is valuable, others will agree. When you believe in the merit of your own words, others will listen. When you are confident, opportunities will magically come your way. People will want to know you. People will want to date you. And people will be jealous of all your good luck.

Confidence From Within

"Do your thing and don't care if they like it." – Tina Fey,
Bossypants

Far too many people make the mistake of basing the way they feel about themselves on the opinions of others. True confidence comes when you believe that you are the same amazing person no matter what anyone else thinks. True confidence comes when you are able to do whatever it is you want to do, no matter what anyone else has to say about it.

You have two options in life. You can either live the life you want, or you can care what other people think about you. Because you can't do both. Sometimes your friends and family will approve of what you're doing, but that won't always be the case. There will come a time when you have to choose whether you want their approval or your own. It's natural to want to fit in, and for that reason most people permit those they know best to have an undue influence on their life. But other people cannot and will not know what is best for you. Only you can. Only you will.

Part of the reason most people aren't very lucky is that they haven't been willing to expose themselves to criticism. They haven't been willing to risk rejection. They would be embarrassed if they tried and failed and so they haven't been willing to try at all. It is true that whenever you try to separate yourself from the pack, you will face pushback, and the more ambitious your plan, the more people will criticize it. Further, the more successful you become, the more people you will encounter who don't like what you're doing. It's impossible to identify a public figure who doesn't have their share of negative press. No matter what it is you're doing, there will be someone who disapproves. To get the life you want, you have to be willing to endure the bad things people might have to say about it. Your opinion is the only one that counts. Trust yourself. If you are following your heart, you are doing the right thing. If you approve of your words and actions and deeds, you cannot go wrong.

There's also something incredibly powerful and attractive about someone who doesn't care what other people think. Not someone who says or does things to be shocking or to gain attention, but one who is truly their own person and who does not feel the need to comply with society's expectations. Confident people are who they are all the time. They don't care if they say something unusual. They aren't concerned about fitting in. People are drawn to them because they wish they could live that way. They too wish that they could do what they wanted without fear of disapproval. People want to be around a confident person in the hopes that some of that confidence will rub off on them. Paradoxically, the less you care about the opinions of others, the higher those opinions will be.

Love Yourself

"To love oneself is the beginning of a lifelong romance." – Oscar Wilde

It's such a cliché: "You have to love yourself before anyone else will love you." But you know what else is a cliché? All those many, many chick flicks and romance novels where a woman with painfully low self-esteem is courted by the man of her dreams. It often involves him saying things like, "You have no idea how beautiful you are," and "I can't believe that no one else can see how wonderful you are." *Bridget Jones's Diary* is the archetype of this genre – a not-very-attractive thirty-something woman finds love with a successful lawyer who likes her "just as she is." It's such a popular fantasy because it gives hope to men and women everywhere who want nothing more than for a gorgeous, fabulous person to come along and tell them that they are worthy of love.

The unfortunate truth is that it doesn't work that way. Even if this mythical person were to come along, a relationship with them could never work. This is the case for one simple reason: if you don't love yourself first, you won't be able to understand how someone so gorgeous and fabulous could love you. Your insecurity would push them away before the relationship had a chance to begin. I know this to be true because I used to be the woman with painfully low self-esteem waiting for my prince charming. I worshiped those books and movies. I wanted desperately for the fantasy to come true, all the while never really believing that it would. After all, who would want to spend the rest of his life with me? It was unfathomable. And so, unsurprisingly, I married the first man who asked. I was so grateful that someone was willing to put up with me. Unfortunately for my ex-husband, I only fell in love with myself sometime after our wedding day. I started to see myself for who I really was. I was smart and pretty and funny. I was a good friend. I had a steady job. I was athletic and loved sports. An excellent catch all around. And when I stopped being so afraid that I would be alone forever, life on my own didn't seem so bad.

For both men and women, it will be very difficult to

date if you can't imagine why someone would want to be with you. You can't wait for someone else to make you feel attractive and special. You have to feel that way about yourself first.

People Believe What You Tell Them

"What kills a skunk is the publicity it gives itself." – Abraham Lincoln

We like to think that there is an absolute quality to our appearance and our character, and that people will evaluate us the way they are going to evaluate us regardless of how we feel about ourselves. We feel that their opinion of us has nothing to do with our own opinion of how we look, or how smart we are, or how much fun we are to be around. For better or worse, this isn't the case. More often than we realize, people will think what we tell them to think about us.

There have been studies demonstrating that people tend to believe what you tell them unless they are motivated to disprove it.[12] If you meet someone new and say something that implies "I am not very interesting," they will take you at your word. Why would they be motivated to disprove that theory? Similarly, if what you say implies that you are fun and energetic and have lots of friends and admirers, people will believe that, too. It's like a Jedi mind trick. If you say something such as, "I didn't think you would like me" or "I'm surprised you find me attractive," you are planting the seed in their mind that they shouldn't have liked you or thought you were attractive. Fortunately, the opposite is true as well. If you respond without surprise, as though you knew all along that they would like you and find you attractive, it will reaffirm in their mind that they've made the right call. When someone compliments you, just say thank you. If someone you like asks you out, just say yes. If someone offers you a big project at work, do not tell them you're under-qualified. When someone has a high opinion of you, don't give them a reason to rethink it.

Further, some people are under the impression that they'll seem amusing or endearing if they poke fun at themselves. There are also those who make jokes about themselves so they can prevent others from making a joke first. Insulting yourself in any way isn't funny. People will believe you even if you're "joking." It may also seem as though you're trying to make others feel bad for you, or that you're fishing for reassurance and compliments. When you insult yourself, you make others responsible for defending you. It's your job to defend yourself.

Remember the section in Belief on the importance of labels. When you describe yourself to others, you are telling them how to label you. Just as basketball players who are drafted early are seen as better basketball players, describing yourself in a positive way can make people see you more positively. Further, recall the study where researchers posed as mental health patients. When they told physicians that they were hearing voices, it led those physicians to view every action taken by the researchers as characteristic of schizophrenia. In the same way, when you say something negative about yourself, it will cause people to see you in a negative light. When you tell someone how to label you, they will see everything you do as fitting with that label. Use this to your advantage, and make sure what you say about yourself is flattering.

Quiet Confidence

"He who has eyes to see and ears to hear can convince himself that no mortal can keep a secret. If his lips are silent, he chatters with his fingertips; betrayal oozes out of every pore." – Sigmund Freud

Even if you never say a negative word about yourself, people will still be able to tell if you have a negative self-image. Confidence is communicated by your body language every bit as much as it is by your words, and body language has the same effect. When you like yourself you invite other people to like you, and when you don't like yourself, you invite other people to pass you by.

In Leil Lowndes's brilliant book, *How to Make Anyone Fall in Love with You*, she describes a segment she once saw on the TV show *20/20*.[13] The segment was about the power of physical attractiveness. It featured two women, one beautiful and the other unattractive. At different times they stood on the side of the highway next to a broken down car. As you'd assume, the men fought over the privilege of aiding the beautiful woman, but couldn't be bothered to help out the unattractive woman. What's interesting about Lowndes's recounting of the story, however, is what she discovered when she watched an interview with the two women at the end of the segment. She found – and verified with a male friend – that when they were just sitting there in freeze frame, the two women didn't look all that different. It was only when you saw them in motion that the difference became clear. The "beautiful" woman was made beautiful by the way she carried herself. She had her shoulders held back, her chest pushed out, and she looked happy and approachable. In contrast, the "ugly" woman was made less attractive by the grimace on her face, her arms crossed in front of her and her general air of misery.

I'm sure you know what confidence looks like when you see it. Right now, picture the most confident person you know. What do they do that makes it so clear that they are confident? I'm guessing that they make eye contact, stand up straight, and walk into rooms like they deserve to be there. It's also easy to envision attributes that betray a lack of confidence. Poor posture. Eyes directed towards the floor. Fidgeting. Nervous tics. Rapid blinking. Blushing. All qualities that say, "Don't look at me."

The way you see yourself is the way the world sees you. It may not seem possible that something as simple as posture and facial expression can make the difference between a beautiful woman and an ugly one, but it seems that it can. If you feel unattractive, and walk and talk as though you're unattractive, other people won't find you appealing either. But if you can look everyone in the eye as they pass you by and say to yourself, "I know you think I'm hot," you might just find that you're right. I know it sounds silly, but it works. Similarly, if you want someone to view you as smart, or athletic, or enthusiastic, you have to see yourself that way first. If you don't look like someone who has those qualities, you'll have a hard time convincing someone that you do. Which brings me to my next point.

Look the Part

"Even I don't wake up looking like Cindy Crawford." – Cindy Crawford

As important as it is to feel good about yourself, all will be for naught if you can't be bothered to put on a clean shirt and comb your hair before leaving the house in the morning. People who don't make an effort with their appearance don't get taken seriously, and they certainly don't get lucky.

One of the most valuable lessons I learned in business school was that people will never buy the product if they don't like the package. It doesn't matter how good your brand of soda is if a person doesn't find the can appealing. Further, even if you get someone to taste it, their negative feeling about the can will translate to a negative feeling about the product. Remember the experiment at MIT where the students didn't like the beer when they knew it had vinegar in it? The same concept applies here. An unappealing package lowers expectations, and our expectations affect our experience. A good tasting soda is a soda that looks like it will taste good.

In the same way people know what a good can of soda looks like, people have an image in mind of what the right person looks like for any job. What does a lawyer look like? What does a personal trainer look like? What does a folk singer look like? If you don't look the part, people will not fairly evaluate whatever it is you have to offer. If you're interviewing for a job in fashion, you can't show up wearing a business suit. And if you're interviewing for a job on Wall Street, you can't walk in wearing the latest fashion. People will see you through the filter of whatever they have decided about you based on your appearance. Just as they will label you based on what you say, they will label you based on how you look. The fashionista might be amazing at finance, but she'll have a hard time being taken seriously.

In your personal life you have to look like someone who might get asked on a date. You have to dress in a way that is attractive to whomever it is you're trying to attract. A lot of women get caught up in what is stylish at the time. Unfortunately, the latest trends often make women look more ridiculous than sexy. Other women might be impressed, but the avant-garde look is only going to stand in your way if you're trying to meet a man. Conversely, some women make the mistake of looking too sexy. Even if you're out at a bar or a club, a man's first impression of you is going to be based on what you're wearing. If you're looking for a husband, don't dress like you're just looking for sex. For the men out there, I would keep it simple. Jeans and a button-down, sweater, or t-shirt work for most informal social occasions. I'd also think twice about wearing any kind of jewelry. But perhaps that's just me.

Everyone has to put effort into the way that they look. Even the most beautiful men and women in the world have to work at it. Sure, Gisele and Tom Brady have a lot of natural beauty to work with, but they still have to have the right haircut and wear the right clothes. Very few of us start with the same raw material as Gisele and Tom, but every one of us has the ability to look our best. I love the show *What Not to Wear*. I highly recommend watching some episodes. You'll get to see women transformed into the best version of themselves, and the difference between the "before" and the "after" is often staggering. It's amazing what some new clothes, a good haircut, and some well-applied makeup can do for a person.

Something else that always struck me about *What Not to Wear* were the excuses people would make for why they previously hadn't put any effort into their appearance. There were the predictable ones: "I'm too busy" or "I just want to be comfortable." But then there were those who didn't see themselves as someone who could be attractive, and so they gave up altogether. They didn't want people to think that they were "trying to be pretty," as though anyone would ever fault someone for wanting to look their best. A lot of us carry around baggage about our appearance that we've acquired over the years. Many of us were teased and criticized as children and teenagers. Or maybe you have the opposite problem – you were a great-looking kid but no longer have the same body you did as an 18-year-old. Don't let these things prevent you from "trying to be pretty." Leave the past in the past. Be the most attractive version of the person you are today. No excuses.

It's also important to look your best *all the time*. When I was growing up my mother always put lipstick on when she left the house, even if she was just going to the supermarket. I'd ask her why and her answer was always the same: "You never know who you're going to meet." You might meet the man or woman of your dreams while shopping for tomatoes. If you're wearing your pajama bottoms and a twenty-year-old Snoopy t-shirt, you'll probably go hide by the broccoli rather than introduce yourself. Further, note that how you look at the supermarket makes the difference between whether this chance encounter is a lucky one or an unlucky one. If you're looking fantastic, you'd be thrilled to come across someone so attractive. But if you're looking like you just rolled out of bed, you might be thinking about how unlucky it is that this person wasn't at the bar last night when you were dressed appropriately.

We assume a lot about people based on how they look. Everything about your physical appearance sends a message, and you need to take control of the message you are sending. Make sure it says: "I am awesome and you should want to get to know me / hire me / go on a date with me."

Confidence 101

"It is better to be looked over than overlooked." – Mae West

You may be wondering where to begin if you aren't feeling particularly confident right now. It can seem daunting to go from wanting to stand in the darkest corner of the room to wanting to be in the spotlight, but it can be done. A lack of confidence can be attributed to a poor self-image, and your self-image is nothing more than the set of beliefs you have about yourself. First and foremost, start by determining what it is that you believe. Are you smart? Are you shy? Are you funny? Are you good-looking? Are you a good person? Do people like you? Are you fun to hang out with? Figure out whatever it is you think you might be lacking, and then work to change that belief.

Let's revisit the four-step belief changing process I outlined in the previous chapter. First, determine where the belief came from. Next, decide what to believe instead, gather evidence for the new belief, and then reinforce the new belief over and over again. The third step will be particularly important when it comes to confidence. Coming up with good evidence to disprove your old beliefs is paramount, and the best way to do that is to actively test your new beliefs. Let's say that you haven't been able to approach attractive women at parties due to your belief that they wouldn't be interested in talking to you. In order to gather evidence for your new belief, i.e. women are happy to talk to me, you're going to have to be brave enough to try it. If it goes well, you've provided yourself with some pretty powerful evidence. It can be difficult at first to try things that you've been afraid to try, but you'll often find that the fear is worse than the reality. Take a few baby steps in the direction you want to go and you will quickly find yourself gaining steam. Focus on what goes well and see any setbacks as a necessary part of the learning process. Believe that you can be confident and you will be.

Nothing Compares to Me

When you compare yourself to others, you're setting yourself up for trouble. There is research that demonstrates that if you think about professors or smart people in general before taking a trivia quiz, you will do better on it than if you hadn't.[14] (Keep that in mind if you have to take an exam any time soon.) But if you think about one smart person in particular, say Albert Einstein, you will wind up doing *worse* on that quiz. If you compare yourself to someone who is better at something than you are, you will feel worse about yourself – and perform worse – than if you hadn't.

If I got my confidence about my appearance from external sources I'd be in trouble. I live near the SoHo area of Manhattan. It's like fashion model central over here. I walk past professional models on the street almost every time I leave my apartment, not to mention the many, many other beautiful women who live in this city. Not a day goes by that I don't see a dozen women who are prettier than I am. But so what? Another woman being beautiful doesn't make me ugly. There's no limit on the amount of beauty in the world.

Don't let someone else's beauty, or intelligence, or humor, or athleticism intimidate you. Everyone is good at something. Everyone has something going for them. If someone is a better soccer player than you, it doesn't make them a better or more valuable person. Focus on doing your best and being your best. And chances are, you're better than they are at something. I'm not suggesting that you see someone with great hair and think, "Oh, well they're fatter than I am," in an attempt to feel better. But it's silly to be intimidated by someone for one quality when we all have so many great qualities.

Further, don't let someone else's success make you angry or jealous. This book is called *All the Luck* because it's about people who seem to have all the luck. I have a friend who saw someone in her life who appeared to be ridiculously lucky. I remember her telling me that she looked at this woman and thought to herself, "Oh, well, she can't be as happy as she seems. Everyone has problems." I hated that. I remember thinking, "Why wouldn't you rather believe it's possible to be that happy?" If someone else has what you want, use that as motivation to go after it. Even better? That lucky person is the best person to go to for advice on how to get there. You know someone that has achieved what you want. He or she can tell you how they did it.

Confidence At Work

"At home I am a nice guy, but I don't want the world to know. Humble people, I've found, don't go very far." – Muhammad Ali

In my professional life, I've come across so many people who work quietly with their noses to the grindstone, hoping that one day someone will take note of their accomplishments. The thing is, if you want to succeed in the workplace, you have to *tell* people about your accomplishments. It all comes down to knowing your worth – or, more accurately, making sure that other people know your worth. Consider employees A and B. Both are great at their jobs. But employee B is better at communicating her value to her boss and co-workers. Who do you think is more likely to get the promotion? Employee B, every time.

I've found that the most effective way to communicate your value is to build a brand for yourself. Make yourself known for having a particular skill set, a skill set you know will be highly valued by your employer. What is it that sets you apart? I used to work with a bunch of statisticians. We were all good at statistics, but I happened to have particularly good communication skills. I was very good at explaining the complicated analyses that we did to people who were unfamiliar with statistics. I knew that my skills in this area were valuable; to advance my career, I needed to make sure everyone else knew it as well. I used every opportunity to drive this point home. In my performance evaluations, I talked about my communication skills. When my supervisors asked what direction I saw my career going, I'd say that I'd like to aim for a position that best utilized my communication skills. When I was lobbying to get put onto high profile projects, I would subtly remind my coworkers how effectively I could communicate in big meetings. When you're talking about the work you do, make sure you're painting a consistent picture. If you do it effectively, you will become known throughout your company for having a particular skill. Obviously, there is a point at which you can go overboard, but far too many people err on the side of modesty and allow their expertise to go unnoticed.

You also need to advocate for yourself. No one is ever going to promote you if you don't ask them to. No one is ever going to give you a raise unless you ask them to. Think about your favorite restaurant. You might love their food, but would you ever volunteer to pay extra for it? You might tip a bit more for great service, but otherwise you're going to pay the price you're asked to pay. You'd probably be willing to pay more if they changed the menu prices, but you're not going to pay more until they do so. You have to ask to get paid more if you want to get paid more. And it'll be a hell of a lot easier to justify a raise and promotion if the powers that be already know what makes you such a great employee.

Confidence is Sexy

Everyone knows what it feels like when you first meet someone great. Your heart is racing, your palms are sweating, there are butterflies in your stomach. If you're lucky, the person you've met is feeling the same way. The question becomes, in the midst of all that anxiety, how are you going to get yourself a date? The answer, of course, is to be confident. If you can stay calm and focus on feeling sexy rather than scared, you can get your target to relax as well. The more comfortable you can get someone to feel, the more likely it is that they'll make a move (or respond well to yours!).

A lot of people have asked me how they can tell if someone likes them. My answer is always the same: I assume everyone likes me. It's not an ego trip, it's a strategy. If you knew for certain that the cute guy you've had your eye on liked you, wouldn't you behave differently than if you didn't? Wouldn't you be much calmer around him? Wouldn't you be instantly more charming because you weren't nervously tripping over your words? Flirting would be easy, because you'd know he wants you to flirt. You'd be less self-conscious, and you wouldn't have to try so hard. I recognize that it takes a lot of confidence to pull off this move effectively. If you're naturally shy, you might have to work your way up to this one, but I assure you it will be worth the effort. Your odds of seducing someone go way, way up if you can go into the situation believing that your crush is already seduced.

Another question I get a lot is how to turn a friendly conversation into something more. You meet someone new, and you're both being polite, but you want to up the flirt factor. I have two fail-safe strategies:

(1) **Sexy eyes.** First and foremost, make lots and lots of eye contact. People that are into each other look into one another's eyes way more often and for much longer than friends or strangers. Extra eye contact can make any conversation feel sexy. It'll work particularly well if you're looking at them like you want to see them naked. I dated someone once who called it my "Are you going to kiss me or what?" look. Exactly. If they kiss you you'll know you're doing it right.

(2) Invade their space. Stand close to them, have lots of inadvertent contact, and find reasons to touch them. Touching is the universal signal for "we are not just friends."

Confidence puts you in the driver's seat because so few people are able to be confident around someone they like. Your target will likely be grateful to you for saving them the effort of doing the seducing.

You'll Love Me Once You Get to Know Me

Once you've met someone you like, confidence is critical to turning that first kiss into a lasting relationship. It takes confidence not to jump right into a relationship (or into bed!). It takes confidence not to say yes to every invitation. And it takes confidence to not settle for less than you deserve. In short: you're a lot more likely to have a successful romantic life if you are confident. Good looks or money might help you along, but for *anyone* it takes confidence to close the deal.

Separate Love and Attraction

"What I'm saying is, chemistry is a place to start, not an end point." – Deb Caletti, The Secret Life of Prince Charming

Love at first sight is such a romantic concept. "I knew she was the one for me from the first moment I saw her." I think love at first sight works wonderfully in retrospect. If you're happily married, go ahead and believe you fell in love at first sight. But if you've just walked into a bar and there's a hot guy standing by the pool table, do not think that you're in love. All you can tell at first glance is whether or not you're physically attracted to someone. Important, yes, but not enough to build a life on. Attraction is a prerequisite for what might follow, but it is nothing more than a prerequisite. You can have a special feeling about someone. You can think that this is someone you *could* fall in love with. But don't think for a second that you can leap frog over all the getting-to-know-you / trust-building / meeting the parents stages that come in between "hello" and "I love you."

People want to be loved for who they are. People want to believe that they are different and special. If you fall in love with someone immediately, they'll know it's not because they're different and special. You couldn't possibly know that yet. They'll know you love them because you wanted to be in love with someone and you figured that they would do. Wait for someone to show you who they are before you love them, or even before you *like* them for that matter. It tends to come off as desperate if you're into someone too quickly. Let them impress you before you make your move.

Don't Bring Him Home

Ladies: do not sleep with a man the first time you meet him. And I don't just mean "don't have sex with him." Do not go home with him. Even if you don't have sex, the first night sleepover sends the same message, "I will go home with just about anyone." I know that may sound harsh, but this is an instance where a little tough love is necessary. There are probably a lot of reasons to wait for sex, but to me it all comes down to knowing a man is interested in you and not just for your vagina. Let's be honest – on a given night, provided enough alcohol is involved, a woman can get pretty much any man to sleep with her. A man doesn't even need to know your name. So long as you're willing, that's enough. But if someone asks for your phone number and arranges to meet you again on *another night* to go on a *real date,* chances are they are interested in more than sex. It's possible that the guy you took home was interested in you for more than sex. But you've shown him that you didn't care if he was or not. You didn't make him prove it. Say what you want about women's rights – you certainly *can* have sex with whomever you'd like. I just wouldn't advise it if you're looking for a relationship. I'm sure we all know someone who had a one-night stand that turned into marriage. Good for them. But being lucky is all about maximizing your odds of success, and you do not maximize your odds when you go home with a man the first time you meet him.

Men: fortunately for you, this rule does not apply. Women will probably even like you more because of it. You have a woman's brain chemistry to thank for that. If a woman has an orgasm her brain will release oxytocin. This handy hormone will make a woman believe that she really likes you, even if she wasn't so sure about you before the sex.

Say No

"An absence, the declining of an invitation to dinner, an unintentional, unconscious harshness are of more service than all the cosmetics and fine clothes in the world." – Marcel Proust

I'm not a big fan of *The Rules*, that crazy book about the games you can play while dating to get someone to chase after you. It might sound like what I'm about to say is recommending that approach, but I assure you that I am not. The advice I'd like to give is something I first heard from Dr. Laura Berman (sex therapist and frequent guest of the Oprah Winfrey show): "Don't play hard to get, be hard to get."

When you first start dating someone, do not see them every time they ask to see you. I don't suggest this because I want you to play games. I suggest it because if you're seeing them every time they ask it means one of two things: either you are changing plans you had already made in order to see them, or you so rarely have other plans that they never conflict. Either of these scenarios will cause nothing but trouble in the long run. If you're changing plans to see him or her it sets a bad precedent. It tells them that what you have going on in your life isn't important to you. It says that you don't value your friendships. It tells them that you're willing to sacrifice yourself for them. Sacrificing yourself for a partner is something you do when you're in a committed, loving relationship, not to schedule a third date. Further, if you have no other plans, it says that you're uninteresting, have nothing going on, and have no other friends or admirers. Have a life of your own, and don't give it up the second you meet someone new.

Have Standards

In Steve Harvey's book *Act Like a Lady, Think Like a Man*, he classifies women as either "sports fish," women that men go after just for fun, or "keepers," women that men want to have a relationship with.[15] This description certainly applies to women, but I think it's applicable to men too – women are just as capable as men of taking advantage of the opposite sex, leading them on, or just generally not treating them right. Women are more likely to use men for companionship than sex, but the same idea applies.

Harvey suggests that it all comes down to "requirements." Sports fish have no requirements, and allow people to treat them however they want, while keepers have high standards and demand to be treated with respect. I'm guessing you won't ever say to someone, "Treat me however you'd like. I'll take whatever I can get." But if you do feel that way, the message will still come through loud and clear. I know far too many women who wait to see what a man wants before they decide what they want.

There's a strange sort of paradox that happens in the dating world: you tend to get what you expect to get. As with most things, what you believe will happen affects what does happen. If you have high expectations and expect to be treated well, you're much more likely to get what you want. Recognize that you have power in the situation, even if it feels like you don't. You always have the ability to say "yes" or "no." If someone offers you something that isn't up to your standards – a casual hook-up rather than a real date – say no. Make it clear to your admirers that if they want to be with you, they have to live up to your expectations.

For the record, I'm not suggesting that you ask someone on your second date whether or not they are looking for a relationship. That will likely send just about anyone running out of the restaurant. At that early stage, how they treat you is what's important. If they regularly schedule dates with you, call when they say they're going to call, and want to spend time getting to know you, you're on the right track. If these things aren't happening and you continue to "see" them anyway (which I'll assume means hooking up), they'll know you have no requirements. Again, there is nothing wrong with having a "casual" relationship if that's what you choose to do. I just don't advise it if you're looking for something more. You're not going to turn a booty call into a boyfriend.

Confidence is a Lifestyle

"For a man to achieve all that is demanded of him he must regard himself as greater than he is." – Goethe

Confidence isn't something you want to turn on and off. It's a much better strategy to be confident all the time. Don't just fire it up if you see someone you're attracted to or you're around someone you think is worth the effort. Get used to being confident. You don't want to test it out when it counts. If you practice being confident in your daily life when nothing important is on the line, it'll be a lot easier in the pressure-packed moments. Make being confident part of who you are. Confidence has the power to enhance every aspect of your life. Not to mention the fact that loving and respecting yourself feels pretty damn good.

Caveat

Arrogance

I think of arrogance as confidence without the charm. The distinction may slight, but it's there. It generally has to do with the way you treat other people. Arrogance is what happens if someone needs people to think that they are wonderful, and will go to whatever lengths are necessary to assure that adoration. True confidence has nothing to do with anyone else's opinion. Those that are truly confident don't care if anyone knows how great they are or not. Further, arrogance generally involves comparisons. Arrogant people need to feel superior to those around them in order to feel good about themselves. Truly confident people, by contrast, aren't troubled by another person's success. Being around gifted people doesn't make them feel less talented.

This may sound at odds with some of the advice I gave about saying positive things about yourself and promoting yourself at work. The important distinction is the context you are in. When someone is asking you about yourself, choose to say positive things, and during your performance evaluation at work, talk about your accomplishments. When you are in a position to describe yourself, don't sell yourself short. But if you're constantly on the lookout for opportunities to insert comments about your greatness, you've gone too far.

(In)Vulnerability

Being confident is not the same thing as never appearing to have flaws. It's quite the opposite, actually. It's being comfortable enough with yourself to show your flaws. It's knowing that you're not perfect and loving yourself anyway.

TENET #3: HAPPINESS

"Happiness is the meaning and the purpose of life, the whole aim and end of human existence." – Aristotle

When people say they want good luck, what they're usually talking about is getting money or love or fame or a great body. They want these things because they believe that having them will make them happy. But what if happiness isn't the outcome of good luck? What if happiness is the *cause* of good luck? As Dr. Deepak Chopra writes in his book *The Ultimate Happiness Prescription*, most people believe happiness comes from what they have in their lives.[16] He feels, however, that these things are the byproducts of happiness and not the source. I love the idea that happiness and positive thinking are what bring what you desire into your life. Be happy first and the good things will follow. Be happy about your luck, and you will be lucky.

Happy Brings More Happy

"We must laugh before we are happy, for fear we die before we laugh at all." – Jean de La Bruyere, Du Coeur

Just about everyone has heard of *The Secret*, the book and movie by Rhonda Byrne, which describes the theory that whatever you want will materialize in your life if you believe that it will.[17] In the book, Byrne goes on to say that belief alone is not enough: you also have to be happy. You have to feel as overwhelmingly happy as you would feel if you already had what you wanted. Byrne suggests that a belief without the accompanying emotions won't go anywhere. You have to emit positive energy to attract positive things into your life.

Whether or not you subscribe to this theory, I am absolutely a believer in the power of having a positive outlook. I've proven to myself that it works. I tried having a positive attitude, all the time, and saw how much better things became. Not just a little bit better, but overwhelmingly, unimaginably better. I realized the extent to which being happy and optimistic had changed my life when I re-read Emily Giffin's book, *Something Borrowed*.[18] I read it once in my early twenties, when I was the epitome of the pathetic single woman, making just about every mistake it is possible to make. I loved the book. I related deeply to the main character, Rachel, an overworked lawyer who was unlucky in love. I didn't think anything of it for years, until one day just after I had turned thirty, when I picked up the book again. I was astounded by how differently I viewed Rachel, the character I had felt such a kinship with just a few years before. I saw clearly how she had created her own bad luck. Her negative attitude was the problem, not random misfortune or her "best friend" who was really more of an enemy. She sat around feeling sorry for herself when it was entirely within her power to change her destiny. I realized, perhaps for the first time, just how much I had been to blame in creating my own bad luck. When I changed my attitude, I changed my luck. Believing that good things would happen brought good things into my life. I'm not suggesting that it was the positive energy I was emitting that created these opportunities. What I can say, however, is that being optimistic changed my behavior. I did things for myself that I wouldn't have done previously. In the past, I wouldn't have pursued a hot guy because I would have been convinced it wouldn't work out. I wouldn't have quit a steady job because I wasn't optimistic about finding another one. I wouldn't have been brave enough to join an all-male ice hockey team because I wouldn't have thought they'd want me there. I had some lucky breaks along the way, but I only came across that luck because I started out in the right direction. I believed things would go well and gave myself the opportunity to see if I was right.

Further, I'm hardly alone in seeing the rewards of having a positive outlook. There have been countless studies demonstrating that optimists have the edge over pessimists in just about every area. Optimists do better in school and at work, perform better at sports, have happier and more successful relationships, are healthier and live longer. If that's not motivation to have a sunnier disposition, I don't know what is.

Happy No Matter What

"Most people are about as happy as they make their minds up to be." – Abraham Lincoln

It can be a difficult concept to grasp at first, but it's a critical one: How happy you are in life has nothing to do with outside circumstances. It may seem as though it's easier to be happy if you have lots of money, or friends, or are devastatingly good looking, but I'm sure you can think of countless examples of people who had all of those things yet still weren't happy. Elvis Presley. Heath Ledger. Marilyn Monroe. Lindsay Lohan. These are people who had many reasons to be happy, and yet weren't. And then there are those who have hardly anything at all and are still blissfully happy. Happiness is a choice. Things alone cannot make anyone happy. If you can have the world at your fingertips and still not be happy, it stands to reason that happiness is more than a mere reflection of the state of the world around you.

There is plenty of research to demonstrate that your circumstances have less impact on your happiness than you might think. As it turns out, having more money won't necessarily make you any happier. Once someone has enough to live comfortably, additional income has little impact on happiness.[19] Further, even major life events have little effect on long-term happiness. Winning the lottery or losing a limb will make you either very happy or very unhappy in the short run. But as demonstrated in a 1978 study of those who had experienced either the lucky or tragic event, both groups were about equally happy a few short months after it occurred.[20] In fact, this finding points to why things cannot make you happy. If a few months after a person wins the lottery, they're just as happy (or unhappy) as they were before, how many things do they need to buy to be permanently happy? People can get stuck in this cycle forever. They buy a fancy house, but a few months later it has ceased to make them happy. Now they need an even bigger house, or a nicer car, or a private plane. It can go on and on because nothing will ever make them happy for very long. People have a remarkable ability to adapt to their circumstances, regardless of whether those circumstances are great ones or terrible ones. Long-term happiness depends much more on your outlook than on your environment.

Knowing that happiness is not based on outside circumstances can be extremely liberating. If you can learn to separate your happiness from possessions and people, you can free yourself from the emotional highs and lows that inevitably occur when your happiness is tied to outside factors. If your happiness is based on something outside of yourself, you have no control over it, and it as always at risk. But once you take charge of your own happiness, you'll know that you can be happy no matter what. How much easier would it be to cope with setbacks if they didn't affect your happiness? What chances would you be willing to take, knowing that win or lose, you can be happy? You don't need a reason to be happy. You can be happy right now if you choose to be.

Happy (Even if You're Not) Together

"The lonely one offers his hand too quickly to whomever he encounters." – Friedrich Nietzsche

Few things cause as much anxiety and distress among people around the world as being unlucky in love. So many feel that they are incomplete until they have a partner, and that a life worth living is only one that is shared with someone else.

We live in a society obsessed with love and marriage. There is an endless array of TV shows devoted to matchmaking and wedding planning. Women in particular are subjected to scrutiny and criticism if they have made it to a certain age without a mate. As Suzanne Schlosberg puts it in her highly amusing book, *The Curse of the Singles Table*:

> In your thirties, you dread taking your place at the Singles Table. Your singleness has started to feel like something more serious than the flue, something chronic, painful, and obscure – like diverticulitis. Deep down you know you haven't done anything to cause your condition, but you know that other people suspect it's your fault, and in your worst moments you start to wonder if they're right.[21]

A wedding ring has become a woman's primary symbol of success, and it's not much different for men. Perhaps men are allowed a few extra years before the whispers and sidelong glances begin, but they are certainly not immune from the pressure to wed. And the pressure isn't just external. So many wait (impatiently) for the day when their Prince Charming (or Princess Charming) comes along to save them from their plight. Many harbor the false notion that once they are in a relationship, all of their dreams will come true and they will never feel sad, lonely or insecure again. No wonder they want to be in one so desperately.

The sad irony is that the more desperately you want a relationship, the more difficult one is to find. The reason for it is this: if you need a relationship to make you happy, you will never be happy in a relationship. Making others responsible for creating your happiness is a losing proposition. Putting the burden of your happiness on the shoulders of someone else is unfair and untenable. Even if a man or woman initially makes you happy, you will keep the pressure on them to continue making you happy day after day after day. People tire quickly under that kind of strain. And if your significant other should make any kind of misstep, it becomes a cataclysmic event. After all, if your entire happiness is tied up in that person, they'd better be perfect. Hardly a recipe for success.

Among those who fervently wish to be in a relationship, many make the mistake of settling for whatever relationship they can find. I certainly did. Relationships are not like lifeboats: any one will not do. The happier you are swimming about on your own, the more likely it is you'll find the best boat for you. If you don't pick someone you're truly in love with, it'll make being single look really good. When I was getting married the first time I remember thinking, "If I'm ever unhappy in my marriage, I'll re-watch every episode of *Sex and the City* and it will remind me how awful being single can be." I, of course, did find myself unhappy, and I followed suit and watched the show. And you know what I saw? How much fun they were having, the freedom they had, the first kisses, the passion. I also saw how focused they were on getting married, and how they seemed to view marriage as some kind of utopia. It's only possible to feel that way about marriage if you've never been married. Being in a bad marriage made me see how many good things there were about being single that I had never appreciated. The years that I was divorced were the only time I ever really enjoyed being single, and not surprisingly that's when I met my husband. Believe me when I say that being single is much, much better than being in a bad relationship. At least when you're single you have the possibility of meeting someone great. In a bad relationship, all you have is the certainty that it will never be good.

I love my life with my husband, Adam. I would never trade it in for another crack at being single. But that's only because my relationship with Adam is so great. There were many things I loved about my single life: I spent more time with friends, I played more hockey, I could flirt with boys, and I always got to watch what I wanted on TV. You give some things up when you get married. I would only have been willing to do that for someone truly worthwhile. Make your goal having a life you would miss if you were with the wrong person.

You must also make peace with your loneliness. One of my favorite thoughts on the subject comes from the book *Dalva* by Jim Harrison: "... each of us must live with a full measure of loneliness that is inescapable, and we must not destroy ourselves with our passion to escape our aloneness."[22] We are all lonely sometimes. Be cognizant of the lengths you are willing to go to escape that feeling. You can't talk yourself into loving someone. If you have to, you don't really love them. And you can't stay with someone just because you're afraid to be single.

The best way to find and keep a relationship is to be happy without one. You can't fake this feeling – people can sense neediness and desperation a mile away. It only works if you really mean it.

Happy Right Now

"Most men pursue pleasure with such breathless haste that they hurry past it." – Soren Kierkegaard

Resist the urge to put off your happiness to some unspecified future date. You see it happen all the time: "I'll be happy when I have more money." "I'll be happy when I lose 20 pounds." "I'll be happy when I meet the right guy." The problem is that when you wait to achieve your goal to be happy, you actually make it harder to achieve. None of us perform at our best if we're not enjoying what we're doing at the time.

I thought about this a lot when watching the most recent Olympic Games. These men and women train their whole lives for the shot at a moment of glory. Do they regret it if they don't win? What if they had sacrificed their happiness for years for this one chance and weren't able to perform on the big day? I suppose it would make them miserable if the training had been miserable. Perhaps it would be worth it if they won, but it still seems a steep price to pay. Further, from my unscientific survey, it appears that those who loved their sport and loved to train were the ones who were the most successful. The perfect example of this was Missy Franklin, the 17-year-old who won five medals, four of them gold, at her first-ever Olympics. Every expert told her that she would need to move to a "serious" training facility if she wanted to be a successful swimmer. But Missy was happy living at home surrounded by friends and family, swimming with her high school team and training with the same coach she'd had since childhood. I remember her saying in an interview that she didn't think she could be successful if she wasn't happy. And it turns out she was right. Happiness and success aren't mutually exclusive, and if you don't have happiness, it's harder to find success.

I know you probably aren't pursuing an Olympic dream, but whatever it is you are after, it's likely just as important to you, and it's just as important for you to be happy along the way. Let's use someone who is dieting as an example. Usually when someone goes on a diet, they adopt some very restrictive eating plan and hard-core exercise program. They don't plan to be happy while they're on the diet. They plan on losing the weight and then being happy. But because they'll be so miserable while dieting, they won't stick with it and will never reach their goal. Someone would be much better off coming up with a program they could be happy with even before the weight comes off.

None of us are going to live forever, and we can't ever know what the future has in store for us. You can't be so focused on preparing for the future that you neglect your happiness today. There are a lot of worthy long-term goals that require hard work and dedication. But you can and must find a way to enjoy yourself along the way. You'll be more likely to get there if you do.

See Things in a Positive Light

"Happiness does not depend on outward things, but on the way we see them." – Leo Tolstoy

When something goes wrong or when you are faced with something you don't want to do, there are two ways to view the situation: "What's great about this?" or "Why does this suck?" In some cases there's an obvious cost/benefit relationship between the action and the outcome. I might not want to go to the gym today, but I can choose to focus on how great I'll look in my bathing suit rather than how much I'd rather be watching TV. In other situations, finding the benefit can take a little effort. Adam and I once got stranded at an airport in Bangkok after missing our flight through no fault of our own. Negotiating with the airline employees, who spoke limited

English, to get us on another flight was a trying experience. To calm us both down I did what has now become a habit: I decided what the best thing about the situation was. Yes, it was frustrating and inconvenient, but we were heading to a glorious, tropical island in Thailand. That was pretty lucky. I'd much rather be annoyed in an airport in Bangkok than not be on vacation. You'll be amazed how quickly you can defuse a situation if you can get yourself and others to focus on the positive.

Optimism 101

If you'd like to work on having a more positive attitude, *Learned Optimism* by Dr. Martin Seligman is an excellent resource.[23] If you're just looking for a few pointers, I'll give you the nutshell version here.

Dr. Seligman's theory focuses on how we respond to problems. He suggests that optimists and pessimists differ in the way they explain why the problem occurred and the effect the problem will have. If something bad happens, pessimists tend to believe the problem is permanent, pervasive, and personal, while optimists believe the opposite. Let's look at these response categories in a bit more detail:

Permanent. This is the belief that the problem will never be solved. Let's say someone screws up a project at work. A pessimist would believe the problem can't be fixed, their reputation is permanently ruined, and that they'll never recover from the mistake. An optimist would believe the situation can be easily resolved and the error soon forgotten.

Pervasive. This is the belief that the problem will affect every area of your life. For a pessimist, a problem at work translates to a fight with a significant other, cancelling plans with a friend, and a drinking binge or other unhealthy response. Optimists are able to separate a problem in one area of their lives from every other area. They are able to leave the work drama at work and come home to enjoy family and friends as much as they always do.

Personal. This is the belief that the problem was caused by the person. A pessimist would think, "I'm so stupid, I'm always screwing things up, I'm terrible at this job." An optimist is more likely to blame an outside factor, like having been distracted by another project or not getting clear enough directions from their supervisor. An optimist does not believe that they are the cause of every situation that goes awry.

Think about your own response to problems. Do any of these response styles sound familiar? They all boil down to one factor: how quickly do you bounce back when something goes wrong? Optimists see a problem and immediately start taking constructive steps towards finding a solution. Pessimists give up quickly or don't bother trying because they don't believe they can fix what went wrong. If you can adopt an optimistic response style, you'll be able to rapidly get back on track and spend less of your life stuck in a difficult situation.

Smile

"It was only a sunny smile, and little it cost in the giving, but like morning light it scattered the night and made the day worth living." – F. Scott Fitzgerald

A smile is a powerful thing. It makes you instantly more attractive and approachable. A smile says, "I like you. I'm happy to see you." A smile is an excellent way to say "Thank you." And the power of the smile doesn't end there – the very act of smiling can make you happy. There have been numerous studies demonstrating that smiling on its own produces positive feelings. The effect is so powerful that Botox injections can be used as a treatment for depression.[24] It seems that if you're physically incapable of frowning, you will be a happier person.

A Zest for Life

"I think happiness is what makes you pretty. Period. Happy people are beautiful. They become like a mirror and they reflect that happiness." – Drew Barrymore

Happiness is a very attractive quality. Happy people are playful and lighthearted, energetic and adventurous, quick to laugh and easy to please. And these qualities are infectious. People are drawn to happy individuals because they too want to laugh and play and forget their concerns and responsibilities.

I'd like you to think about how much luckier you stand to be simply by being happier. When you talk about your life with enthusiasm, it makes people want to be a part of it. If you make what you're doing sound exciting, people will want to join you. You will make friends more easily and get more dates. Further, people will think more highly of everything you do because your enthusiasm will make it sound so appealing. People will get excited about your business and want to invest or buy things from you. In my old workplace, people frequently commented on what a positive attitude I had. The quality of my work may have been equivalent to that of others, but when I handed in a project with a smile on my face, it was inevitably valued more highly. Again, the work I did wasn't any different, but my attitude was better, and so they liked it more. People think more highly of happy people. People like being around happy people. When you approach everything as though you know it'll be fun, you'll attract a crowd of people wanting to come along for the ride.

Shiny Happy People

"Happiness quite unshared can scarcely be called happiness; it has no taste." – Charlotte Brontë

Take a moment to consider your close friends and family. When you see them, do you have fun? Do they make you feel good about yourself? Do they have a positive outlook on life? Does anyone criticize you? Does anyone "tease" you in a way that isn't funny? Is there anyone that doesn't support your decisions? Either by choice or by chance, many of us have wound up with people in our lives who make it hard to be happy.

There are two factors to consider when thinking about the people you know: whether they support you or criticize you, and whether their attitude is positive or negative. Hopefully, everyone you know is positive and supportive, but chances are that isn't the case. Criticism and negativity are not things you should invite into your world. It's a lot harder to be confident and happy if you are regularly surrounded by people who bring you down. It's the difference between paddling with the current or against it. Those closest to you can either help you along, or they can hold you back. Don't let them hold you back.

Anyone that criticizes you does not deserve a place in your life. Someone doesn't have to agree with you all of the time. A good friend will tell you if they think you are making a mistake. But they will do it because they love you and honestly want you to be happy, and not to make you feel bad about yourself. Often those who are critical believe that they are doing it out of love, but if what they are saying is hurting you, it's not helpful. There is also a question of frequency. If someone doesn't agree with what you're doing, they can, in the kindest possible way, tell you once. If they repeat their criticism over and over, it is no longer constructive.

And then there are those who are always negative. Some people are cesspools of negative energy. Nothing is ever right and there is always something to complain about. They'll never be pleased with anything. If you know someone like this, you'll know what I'm talking about. You can try all you like, but you'll never make them happy. All they will do is suck the positive energy out of you when you're in their presence. They won't want to see you be happy. They'll think it's inconsiderate that you're so happy when they're so miserable. They'll make you feel silly for being optimistic. They'll predict nothing but doom and gloom for you because that is all they are able to see. All good reasons to stop spending time with them.

I know that there will be people you can't easily cut out of your life. They could be parents, or siblings, a spouse, or anyone else you need to stay in contact with. If you can't avoid interaction, the best thing to do is try to improve the relationship. The first step is to communicate clearly that you are not happy with the current state of affairs. Many times when we're upset with someone, we wrongly assume that the other person knows we are upset. It's not fair to be upset with someone until you've expressed your feelings and have given them a chance to respond. If they respond positively, and are willing to work with you on improving your relationship, then great. Any relationship can improve if both parties are willing to put in the effort. However, if they ignore your concerns and continue to behave in a way that is unacceptable to you, you may have to make the difficult decision to cut them out of your life, even if they are family or a close friend.

Soothe Yourself

"Happiness is like those palaces in fairytales whose gates are guarded by dragons: We must fight in order to conquer it." – Alexandre Dumas

When something goes wrong in your life, it helps to have a plan in place for how to get back to being happy. Make a list of things you can do to put yourself in a better mood. As a starting point, I'll share my list with you. This is what makes me happy:

- Music. I have a "happy" playlist. The B.o.B song, "Magic," is my favorite.

- Going for a walk, particularly if the sun is out. Sunshine always helps.
- Shopping. Living in NYC, this is usually what my walks turn into.
- Hugging my husband.
- Hanging out with my girlfriends.
- Bubble baths.
- Reading, particularly if it's something that could be described as "brain candy." I love romance novels.
- Hockey. Playing or watching, but preferably playing. It's impossible for me to play hockey and think about anything but what's happening on the ice. Plus, hitting people is a great way to get some aggression out! (Technically it's against the rules, but a little "incidental contact" never hurt anyone.)

If I'm being honest, "having a glass of wine" is pretty high up on my list, but I would have felt irresponsible putting it there. I think it goes without saying that self-medicating with food or alcohol on a regular basis is a bad idea. A really, really bad idea. Part of the reason to have a list is to know where to turn for happiness that doesn't involve food or alcohol. I'll remind myself of that the next time I reach for the Sauvignon Blanc.

Obviously, if something truly tragic has occurred in your life, or you are struggling with depression, it will take more than a few walks in the sunshine to put things right. If this is the case, I would strongly suggest that you seek professional help, such as a grief counselor or psychiatrist.

Caveat

Empathy

Having a positive outlook doesn't mean you can't empathize with other people. People in your life are going to be negative on occasion and complain about things and be frustrated, pessimistic, et cetera. It's not a good idea to suggest to a person who is upset that they should just be happy all the time. Comfort them. Allow them to bitch and complain. Tell them that you understand why they are upset. You can tell them all about how great having a positive outlook has been for you on another day when they've calmed down.

Bad Days Are Okay

"You know, Hobbes, some days even my lucky rocket ship underpants don't help." – Bill Watterson

Don't be angry with yourself if you have a bad day. I used to get frustrated when something bad would happen. I would be upset about what happened, plus I'd be upset that I was unhappy, knowing how important it is to have a positive attitude. I believed that because I was in a bad mood, good things were less likely to happen. It was a double whammy. I wanted to be positive, but it meant having to ignore the upset, disappointed feelings that I had when things went wrong. Sometimes what I would do is allow myself a set amount of time to indulge in all those negative feelings. I'd allow myself to wallow for twenty-four hours and then get back on track. If you're feeling upset, give yourself a break.

TENET #4: FOCUS

"You got to be careful if you don't know where you're going, because you might not get there." – Yogi Berra

      If you want to be lucky, it would be a good idea to know what kind of luck you're looking for. Looking for luck might seem like a strange idea, but it boils down to this: it's really hard to get what you want if you don't know what that is. Luck can do a lot of things for you, but it can't tell you what to want.

Mirror, Mirror

      My favorite magical object in J.K. Rowling's *Harry Potter* series is the Mirror of Erised. Harry comes across the mirror in the first book of the series, *Harry Potter and the Sorcerer's Stone*. In it he sees his parents, who died when he was a small child, and the family he never knew. It's only later in the book that the reader discovers what the mirror is: a reflection of "the deepest, most desperate desire of our hearts."

Obviously, one can never bring back lost loved ones, but I was enthralled by what this mirror represented – a way to see what it is that you want more than anything else in the world. Not what you should want, or what you want to want, but what you would wish for if you could have anything. Do you know what it is that you want most in the world? It seems a simple question, but often it's not. So many of us hide our deepest desires because we believe there is no way we could ever have them. And if we know we can't have them, why torture ourselves by continuing to want them? But what if you could have them? What if you could have anything?

I had been married to my ex-husband for little more than a year when I first read about this magical mirror, and I immediately knew what I'd see. I would see myself married to someone that I truly loved. Not to the husband I had but to someone else entirely. It wasn't a comforting notion as a relative newlywed to know that the most fervent desire of my heart was to be married to another man. I didn't have a particular man in mind, but I knew the way I wanted to feel and the kind of relationship I wanted to have, and I wasn't getting that with husband number one. I spent months pretending that wasn't what I really wanted, months where I tried to convince myself that I wanted to work on my marriage and find a way to be happy with the husband I had. But that's the cruel beauty of the mirror; it will only show you what you *truly* want. Every time I thought about that mirror I knew what I would see.

I'm continually amazed by how few people know what they want. You have to know what you want, and I don't mean the "realistic" wants, like a 5% salary increase, or a weeklong vacation in the Caribbean. What would make you truly happy? What would make you leap out of bed in the morning, instead of hitting the snooze button five times? What would you do if you didn't have to do anything? If you had ten million dollars and never had to work another day in your life, how would you fill your days? Often people think they'd love a life filled with nothing but rest and relaxation, but you'd be amazed at how quickly you might be bored out of your mind. Everyone needs something to inspire them, something that doesn't feel like work. And once you find your inspiration, you might discover that there is a way to turn what you love to do into a career. Or maybe, like me, your deepest desire is for something less tangible, like a great relationship or some close friends. When you know where it is you want to go, you can start finding a way to get there. You can't have the life you've always wanted until you know what that life would be.

A Clear Vision

"Imagination is everything. It is the preview of life's coming attractions." – Albert Einstein

Deciding what it is you want most is like coming up with the big picture; having a clear vision is filling in the details. Let's say your dream is to become a wind surfing instructor. What would that look like? Where would you live? What kind of skills would you need to have? What would you do on an average day? What kind of people would you meet? The more specific you can make the image of what you want, the more compelling that image will become to you. Visualization goes hand-in-hand with belief. If you can see yourself getting what you want, if you can see yourself living the life you want, you will make it much easier for yourself to believe that it's possible. Remember what we said in the chapter on Belief: if you don't believe something will happen for you, you won't have the motivation to go after it. You'll sabotage yourself before you even start if you can't picture yourself with the prize in hand at the end of the race. See yourself experiencing the success you want. See it every day and know you're going to get there.

Further, visualization can be used as more than a motivational tool. Top athletes and professionals in a number of fields have been using visualization for years to enhance performance. The idea is that if they can rehearse the actions they need to take in their mind, they will be able to execute these actions when it counts. Imagining yourself in a specific situation has a physical effect. Studies have shown that your muscles respond as though you're actually performing the activity even if you are only rehearsing it in your mind. You can physically prepare yourself to succeed by visualizing the specific action it would take to achieve the best result. It might seem as though this technique would only valuable if you're planning on running the 100-meter sprint, but being mentally prepared to take action can be useful in any number of situations. When you have mentally rehearsed doing whatever it is you want to do – waterskiing, flying a plane, asking out the hot woman from the dentist's office – you'll be much more likely to succeed when you do get a chance. Having already experienced it in your mind will reduce the anxiety you will feel in the moment. Once you've seen the story have a happy ending, all you have to do is play out the script you've written.

Focused Power

"Nothing interferes with my concentration. You could put an orgy in my office and I wouldn't look up. Well, maybe once." – Isaac Asimov

While you might have goals for more than one area of your life – lose 20 pounds, start a business, take up skiing and make new friends, for example – it will help if you chose to focus on one at a time. I truly believe that if you make something your first priority and you're willing to do whatever it takes to get it, you can have and do anything you want. As I mentioned in the first section of this chapter, there was a time when finding a satisfying relationship with someone I loved was my first priority. Most people feel that finding love is something that you can't control, and that love exists exclusively in the realm of luck. I don't agree. It takes a bit of luck to come across the right person, but there are many things you can do to increase your odds of coming across that person. There are also many things that happen between a first meeting and forming a relationship that you have the power to control. At the time, having just gone through a painful divorce, I was hardly feeling confident in my ability to make a relationship work. So I did what I knew I could do. I headed straight to the library and Amazon.com and got as many books as I could on how to find and keep a happy relationship. And while I was studying up on dating and relationship strategies, I joined every kind of co-ed team sport I could find. During my divorced years I played ice hockey, street hockey, roller hockey, beach volleyball, football and basketball. I met a lot of good friends on those teams, and yes, that is how I met Adam. I made love my priority and it worked. Even if you're not an athlete, there are plenty of ways to meet potential partners in an organized fashion. Take a wine tasting course or join a sky diving club. Try online dating, or ask friends to set you up with someone.

This strategy can be used for just about any goal. Once you know what you want, there are countless ways to go after it. Find out what it takes to get what you want. Seek out some people who have already accomplished what you would like to accomplish and ask them how they did it. Read books written by experts in the field. Take a class that will teach you the skills you need. Seek professional help, like consulting a nutritionist if you want to lose weight or a tennis pro if you want to improve your game. Find out what the first steps are and then take them. Start moving in the right direction and continue to gather information as you work toward your goals.

Find the Right Motivation
"We only do well the things we like doing." – Colette

Just about everyone thinks that money is a wonderfully motivating factor, but it isn't really. It is in the sense that we know we need it, so we know we have to get up and go to work every day. Keeping a roof over one's head can be pretty motivating. But in and of itself making money isn't fulfilling. It's not a calling. You can be passionate about what money can do for you, but it's difficult to be driven to succeed if money is your only objective. There are a lot of ways to make money, and you will always be better off – and likely even make more money – if you're doing something that you love.

In social psychology there is a theory that we can be motivated by factors that are either "intrinsic" or "extrinsic."

Intrinsic motivation refers to doing something because you want to do it, because you enjoy doing it. Extrinsic motivation refers to doing something because you want the benefit of doing it, but not because you enjoy doing the thing itself. You are intrinsically motivated to read a book if you love to read. You are extrinsically motivated if your teacher is making you read a book and you'll fail the class if you don't. There are a couple of problems with extrinsic motivation. First, when we view an activity as a means to an end, it takes the joy out of the activity. You'll know you're only doing it for the payoff. Even if it was something you initially enjoyed doing, the activity will become associated with the reward, and if the reward is removed you'll lose interest in the activity. There was a classic study done with preschool children who drew pictures with markers.[26] They observed how much the kids enjoyed coloring with markers initially, and later started rewarding them for their drawings. When the rewards stopped, the kids stopped coloring, even if they had loved to color at the start of the study.

Second, you'll never perform a task as well if you're extrinsically motivated. For creative pursuits in particular, the more motivated you are by the money, the worse your product is going to be. You can't want to be a writer or a director or a musician for the money and expect to produce anything exceptional. Your desire to create has to come from within to provide true inspiration. And if you're in business, you have to love what you're doing or love what you're selling to find compelling motivation. When you're following your heart, working doesn't feel like work. You'll know when you're doing what you're meant to do when you can happily spend hours and days absorbed in your work and have to be torn away from it. You'll work longer and harder at something you love than you

ever will at something that's a means to an end. You can hardly
help but be more successful at something you're driven to do
out of desire than something you only do for the paycheck. And
if you do pursue something that causes you to take a pay cut,
the sense of fulfillment you will achieve will more than make up
for it.

Look Where You're Going

*"Skate to where the puck is going and not to where it's been." –
Wayne Gretzsky*

You will move in the direction that you are looking. In
his book, *Awaken the Giant Within*, Anthony Robbins illustrates
this with his experience driving racecars.[27] If you lose control of
the car, the obvious tendency is to look at the wall that you are
barreling towards. But in order to pull yourself out of the skid,
you have to keep your eyes on the road. If you focus on what
you're afraid of – i.e. the wall – you'll crash right into it.

So many people spend their life focused on what they
don't want. "I hate being single" or "I hate being fat." If you are
focused on what you don't want, you are more likely to keep
what you don't want in your life. Let's take being overweight as
an example. If you are focused on how unhappy you are about
yourself, you will constantly feel sad and frustrated. All that
negative energy will likely send you running for the cupcakes in
an attempt to feel better. And then, of course, you start the
cycle all over again.

This is why having a clear vision of what you want is so
important. It's very difficult to stay motivated if all you can see

is the amount of work you're going to have to do, or how long it's going to take to get there, or how upset you are with the way things are right now. You need something to focus on when you're tired and discouraged. Don't see your doubts, don't see your anxieties, and don't see the daily drudgery that may be required to accomplish your goals. See yourself looking fabulous at your goal weight. Feel how good it will feel when you finish graduate school or when you've made your small business successful. If you're saving to buy a beach house, put a picture of it on the wall where you can see it every day. Remind yourself of your motivation as often as you can. Look in the direction you want to go.

People also have a tenancy to focus on bad things that might happen in the future. They worry about getting sick, or losing their job, or fighting with their spouse. Once again, if you focus on where you don't want to go, that is the direction in which you are most likely to head. Let's use the fear of getting sick as an example. Stress and anxiety make it much more likely that you will contract an illness. They impair your immune system and wreak long-term havoc on your body. Fear of disease *can cause disease*. If you're afraid of losing your job, you might behave in an anxious and paranoid way at work. It might cause your boss to question whether you can handle the job, and your name might come up first if layoffs come around.

You have a couple of options in life: you can look around and see all the amazing things you're moving towards, or whatever it is you don't like about your current circumstances. If you don't have an ideal scenario in your head, your default focus will be on what you don't want. Know where you're going and keep your eyes on the road.

Caveat

Fantasy versus Focus

There is a difference between fantasy and focus. A fantasy is when you want to be a rock star and have no musical talent. Focus is when you want to be a rock star and you've played the guitar your entire life and have spent countless hours practicing with your band. A focus is a fantasy that you're willing to *work towards*. You have to be willing devote yourself to pursing your focus. You have to be willing to work hard to achieve it. If those things aren't the case, you haven't found your focus.

Delayed Focus

There may be times when it's not possible for you to follow your dream. Let's say you have a medical condition and can't risk losing your health insurance or you need a steady paycheck to support an elderly parent. Even if you can't pursue your passion, it doesn't mean you can't succeed at whatever you're currently doing. Let that be your aim: get the most out of your present situation, whatever that may be. My husband wasn't following his dream when he was working because he wanted me to be able to stay home and write this book. But he made major strides in his career nonetheless. He negotiated for the best possible salary and the most favorable working conditions – leaving early Fridays, working from home, etc. Even if you have to continue a job you don't love, there is no reason you can't focus on making that job as rewarding as it can possibly be.

Focus on Love

"To keep a lamp burning, we have to keep putting oil in it." – Mother Teresa

If you are married or in a serious relationship, your partner must always, always, always be your first priority, no matter what. A good relationship won't work any other way. You must find a way to manage your focus in such a way that it does not become more important than your spouse. Some people think they can put their relationship on hold while they go to law school or train for a sport or pursue any other goal outside of their relationship. Lasting relationships require a lot of time, energy and attention. You can't hit the pause button on a relationship and think you'll be able to pick up where you left off several months or years later. If you're currently single and pursuing a goal that requires all of your attention, don't try looking for love at the same time. If you're already in a relationship – or want to be in one – you have to make time for it. One of my married friends found herself overwhelmed with classwork and studying when she started dental school. In order to fit quality time with her husband into her schedule, she would come home and have dinner with him every night before returning to her books. You must find a way to keep your relationship alive, even while you are focused on another goal.

Tunnel Vision

There is a point at which you can become too focused on something. You can't let your focus on one aspect of your life lead you to ignore all others. While we're on the subject of love, a classic example is the bride who is so consumed with wedding plans that she's blinded to all the problems she's having with her fiancé. (Might have some personal experience with that one.) Further, many let their dedication to their jobs cause them to neglect their health. You have to keep the big picture in mind. Balance is key. The best wedding in the world won't fix what's wrong in your relationship, and getting the big promotion at work won't do you any good if the stress gives you a heart attack.

TENET #5: BRAVERY

"Fortune favors the bold." – Latin Proverb

"Fortune favors the bold" has long been one of my favorite expressions. Its message is simple: if you want to be lucky, you have to be brave. Why is that the case? Gambling is the perfect way to illustrate this. If you want to win anything in Vegas, you have to place a bet. If you want to give yourself an opportunity to win, you have to risk something. You have to accept the possibility that you could lose and take the chance anyway. In any given situation, your luck might be good, or it might be bad. But those that take the most chances give themselves the most opportunities to win, and the more chances you take, the better you get at taking them. Bad luck can turn into good luck if you can learn from your mistakes and make a better bet the next time.

Aim High

"Life shrinks or expands in proportion to one's courage." – Anaïs Nin

I am of the belief that how far you go in life is a direct reflection of how far you are willing to go. Most people aren't very brave; they set goals for themselves that don't require a lot of courage. Often, though, these are the same people that look at those with incredible lives and wonder how they got so lucky. Just as you can't be jealous of someone who wins the lottery if you never buy a ticket, you can't be jealous of someone with a fabulous, exciting life if you aren't willing to do what it takes to get one.

Lucky people give themselves an opportunity to be lucky. They know what they want and they go after it. More to the point, they go after something worth having. They aim high. In the chapter on Focus, I talked about knowing what kind of luck you're looking for. I also noted that there is a difference between a fantasy and a focus: A focus is a fantasy you're willing to work towards. You get to choose whether what you work towards is something inspiring and amazing, or something ordinary but easy to achieve. The more extraordinary the goal, the more bravery it will take to attain it. There's nothing scary about climbing small hills, but if you want to scale Everest, it's going to take some nerve. And just like those that climb Everest, you are going to have to put yourself in situations that are unfamiliar and uncomfortable, and you're going to have to endure moments when you're terrified and want nothing more than to turn back. But you have to keep going. Only those who are willing to make the journey can get to the top.

We live in a culture that values hard work and diligence, but there has never been enough emphasis placed on the value of taking chances. As a society we tend to view risk takers as reckless, yet just about anyone who has ever been wildly successful has taken a risk. Every entrepreneur has to bet on himself and his own idea. Every musician has to be brave enough to risk rejection and ridicule whenever they play a gig. Every politician that runs for election has to risk losing. Hard work and diligence are important factors in any success story, but you can't get very far without taking a risk.

Bravery and confidence are also closely linked concepts. If you don't have a high opinion of yourself, you're unlikely to wager very much on your ability to succeed. To do something really brave, you have to be confident in your chances. You have to believe that your ideas and your talent are worth betting on. Aiming high requires believing that you deserve to be high. You are the one who puts the limits on what you believe you are capable of, and you decide how far you think you can go. Decide to go far.

Change Course

"A man can stand almost anything except a succession of ordinary days." – Goethe

Everyone's life is on course for something. What is the destination of the train you're on today? If you continue to live your life exactly as you are right now, where will you be in five years? In ten years? In twenty years? Imagine your future in great detail. What will you look like? What will your job look like? Where will you be living? Are you single? If you're in a relationship, what does your relationship look like? Is the life you are heading towards all that you hoped it would be? If not, change course.

Every decision you make changes the track your life is on. It either moves you closer to or further away from where you want to go. You might think you're moving along in a straight line, but we're all either rising up or sinking down. If you know you need to make some changes in your life but continue not making them, you're going downhill. It might be such a slow and steady decline that you can't see it or feel it, but you'll know you've moved when you look out the window in a few years and see how far you've fallen. Bad habits and poor decisions take their toll over time. I think about this whenever I encounter a smoker or someone who is morbidly obese. The train they're on is speeding towards a hospital bed. No one wants to go there, and yet that is where they will be if they don't get on a different train.

Health problems aside, how many people are on a train moving towards a joyless and unsatisfying life? If you hate your job now, what are the chances that you're going to like it any better ten years from now? And what will ten years of suffering through day after day of unsatisfying labor have done to your spirit? People who have had a near-death experience have a very interesting perspective on life. They know for sure something that the rest of us tend to forget: each day is a gift. No one has guaranteed you a long and healthy life. You can't take for granted that you're going to have 85 or more years with which to accomplish your goals. You have to start now. You need to do what you have to do to be happy today. Not tomorrow, but today. Each particular day may not seem so valuable to you when you seem to have so many of them. But what if you didn't? How differently would you be living your life if you didn't have as much of it left as you thought? You wouldn't want to waste it doing something you hate.

You might think you don't have a choice. This is why believing that you have options is so critical. You might feel that you have to stay at your job for the stability, the pension, the paid vacation days, or any number of reasons. Or that you have to stay married for the sake of the kids. It's just not true. You always have options. If you choose to look for another way, you will always be able to find one. Further, it's critical that you make yourself aware of the consequences of not changing directions. Each day on its own might not seem so bad. But what is the accumulated cost of all of those mediocre days? What is the value of that kind of life? Isn't it possible to do better? Enduring is not enjoying. If you're not moving towards what you want, you're moving away from it. Start going the right way.

It can be difficult to change directions when you've been heading down one path for a long time. The longer you've lived the life you have, the deeper the tracks you've created for yourself will be. The good news is that even a small change can reap a huge reward over time. What you want might seem very far off in the distance, but it's not. Time flies, and the older we get, the quicker it seems to go. Your future will rapidly be upon you whether it's one you want or one you don't. Time magnifies the results of your actions whether they are productive ones or destructive ones. Even if you write only fifty words a day, eventually you will have a novel. Even if you exercise for only twenty minutes a day, eventually you will improve your fitness level. Time can work either for you or against you. You are going to get somewhere eventually. Make sure it's a place you want to be.

There will be times, of course, when a small change just isn't enough. There will be instances in which all that will do is a dramatic about-face. These types of changes can require the most bravery, but they can also produce the greatest rewards in the shortest amount of time.

It is never too late to make a change. It might be hard. It might take a long time. But once you've taken the time and done the work you will be so happy you did.

In With the New

"As many people die from an excess of timidity as from bravery." – Norman Mailer

There are those who view any kind of change as a risk. But is that valid? Not all new things are scary. There are no dire consequences that await you if you try sushi for the first time or join a new book club. Doing new things can be a great way to ease yourself into bravery. It's a risk-free way to become more familiar with feeling unfamiliar. Having the experience of being temporarily uncomfortable in order to discover something new and wonderful can be very rewarding. You can begin to prove to yourself that taking a chance or making a change, even in the smallest, safest possible way, can really pay off. Try something, anything, that makes today different from yesterday. Get lunch from a different restaurant. Watch something different on TV. Take a different route to work. When you try that new restaurant and find a new dish you absolutely love, you will get your first taste of how new can be better.

Many people associate "different" with "bad." Different can be good or bad, but you'll never know until you try it. Remember the important role played by your expectations. If you think everything new will be bad, then it will be. But it needn't be, and you are likely depriving yourself of many good things simply by avoiding them. As they say, "you don't know what you're missing." I love the *Harry Potter* books, as I know many, many other people do. They have provided me with countless hours of joy, but I have friends that won't read them because they think they won't like them. My argument is always, "How can you know you won't like them if you haven't tried them?" You can't form an opinion about something you've never tried. There are so many amazing things out there that you could be missing out on. One of my cousins just tried Indian food for the first time and now he eats it almost every night. A great new thing that would drastically improve your quality of life could be just around the corner.

Trying something new can feel uncomfortable at first. When you try your first Zumba class or sign up for a rock climbing course there will be moments when you don't know anyone or you don't know what you're supposed to do. But being new is a temporary condition. Everyone was new at some point. Soon enough the new will be old and you'll be telling all your friends how much you're enjoying your new activity.

People build up the fear of new things in their head. Fear of the unknown is just an excuse to stay planted in your comfort zone. If you're looking for luck, your comfort zone is the last place you're going to find it. You need to learn to evaluate what is truly risky and what is simply fear. At the end of the day, nothing is riskier than never trying anything new.

What's the Worst that Could Happen?

"Courage is knowing what not to fear." – Plato

No, really: What's the worst that could happen? When you're thinking about taking a risk, determine what the worst possible outcome would be. What would it look like if everything went wrong? It's important to do this for a couple of reasons. The first is that more often than not you will find that the worst-case scenario really isn't that bad. Second, if the worst-case scenario really *is* that bad, don't take the risk.

Start by defining your fear. If you want to quit your steady job to travel for a year, chances are that you would be concerned about finding a new job when you get back. Do some research. Is it possible that your current employers would take you back? How difficult is it to find work in your industry? If you look for a new job, how long do you think it would take to find one? How much would you need to have saved to be able to support yourself over that period of time? If you had to, could you move in with your parents? Is there any way you could make some money while you're looking for a new position? If you look, you might find that your worst-case scenario actually isn't so difficult to manage.

When I was writing this book, my worst-case scenario was that no one would like it and I'd never sell a copy. But I would tell myself: "Even if it's not successful, at least I'll have written a book. I will be proud of myself for that accomplishment." I had always wanted to write a book. Whether or not it succeeded, I'd have accomplished a goal I set for myself a long time ago. And if the book failed, I would have had the experience of writing it to help me in writing the next one, along with some valuable feedback. Sure, it would suck if no one liked my book. But it wouldn't have been the end of the world, and it wasn't a good enough reason to not write it.

If your worst-case scenario involves something much worse than moving back in with your parents for a few months, or facing some temporary failure or rejection, it might not be worth taking. There's an old gambling adage that says, "Don't bet the grocery money." If a risk is going to devastate you financially, to a point from which it would be very difficult to recover, it's not worth taking. The fear that it wouldn't work out would be overwhelming. If there is a very real possibility that you could be sleeping on a park bench in the near future, your behavior would likely become frantic and desperate. You can't perform at your best under that kind of stress. It may be helpful to decide ahead of time how much time or money you are willing to devote to a plan before calling it quits. If you can afford to invest $5,000 in your small business but any more than that would put you in financial peril, make sure to cut yourself off at the $5,000 mark. Or you might decide ahead of time how many years you'll spend pursuing a career in acting before going back to school. Having a time limit might help assuage any fear that you'll be jobless forever.

Lastly, give yourself a chance. Planning for the worst case does not mean you should behave as if the worst has happened already. If you want to be an actor, at least *try* to succeed at acting before you head into your backup plan. You might think your dream will go away while you're busy studying finance, but I find that unlikely. I think it's much more likely you'll still want to be an actor two years from now, only by then you'll be $100K in debt from paying for business school.

What's the Worst That Could Happen (Emotionally)?

"The bitterest tears shed over graves are for words left unsaid and deeds left undone." – Harriet Beecher Stowe

For many people, the worst thing that could happen to them isn't losing money or having to move back in with their mother, but the emotional toll of failing to reach a goal. They know how upset they would be if things went wrong, so to them no risk is ever worth taking. It's important to separate the emotional worst-case scenario from the practical worst-case scenario. As I said in the previous section, if failure would leave you homeless and penniless, perhaps don't take the risk. But if the worst thing that happens in a situation is that you have to endure some temporary embarrassment or disappointment, you have no excuse.

The emotional response to failure is something you can control. It might look like someone who is able to flirt with lots of girls, get shot down, and keep on going with a smile on their face is just lucky. It might seem as though they were born that way, and that it's easy for them. You might curse your bad luck for making you shy and terrified of being rejected. But you can change your luck. You can change your response to failure, and in the process, make risks look less risky.

The best way to go about this is using some techniques from a book I mentioned in the Happiness section called

Learned Optimism.[23] Optimists are able to separate the moment from the big picture. They are able to experience an instance of failure without feeling as though they are a failure. They know that one failure doesn't mean their whole life is ruined, and they feel confident that they can either improve the situation or have it work out for them the next time. You are the one who gets to decide how to feel when things go wrong. You can train yourself to respond to failure with resolve and positive expectations about the future, and once you do, you can take more risks, confident that you will be able to bounce back quickly if things don't work out.

It's important to recognize how much you stand to lose – and how unlucky you stand to be – if you are not able to overcome your fears. Momentary rejection is nothing compared to a lifetime of regret. In most cases, what you might lose is minimal compared to what you could gain. If you have a crush on someone and you're unwilling to do anything about it, you could be sacrificing a lifetime full of love and happiness with the person of your dreams, all to avoid a few moments of embarrassment. Sure, you'll be disappointed if it doesn't go well, but it's the only way you can get what you want. Doing nothing is worse than getting rejected, and trying nothing is worse than failing. At least if you are rejected or you fail you will know where you stand and can move on with your life. If you never try, you can never fail, but you can't possibly win, either. It is worth overcoming your fears. Like most goals, begin by believing it's possible to overcome them and go on from there. Start small and begin to prove to yourself that you can do it.

Do Your Homework

"By failing to prepare, you are preparing to fail." – Benjamin Franklin

If you're going to take a risk, you want to give yourself the best possible odds of having that risk pay off. As I hope I've convinced you, success and failure are not up to pure chance. There will always be factors that are under your control, and by controlling those factors, you can give yourself a better chance of success. You can't take a risk without proper preparation and hope for luck to bail you out. You have to do your homework.

Let's say you want to start a small business in your hometown. You could go ahead and lease a location and hope for the best, but that's probably not the smartest plan. If you were serious about success, you'd head to the town and investigate which businesses are the most successful. Assess your competition and determine whether there will be a big enough market for your goods or services. Figure out how much money you might be able to make. At the end of your evaluation, you should know what you can do to maximize your chances of success, or, alternatively, discover that that your chances of success are too slim to justify the risk.

For whatever it is you want to achieve, there is a way to research the best way to do it. There is always someone you can go to for advice, and self-help books are available for just about any topic. Want to learn how to pick up women? There's a book for that. Want to learn how to put together an effective resume? There's a book for that. Want to lose some weight? There are approximately eight million books for that. Learn from those who have been there and done that. Understanding how the lucky got lucky is the best way to do it yourself.

It's particularly important to do your homework if you're taking a risk in an area that you are unfamiliar or uncomfortable with. You don't want to jump into the deep end of a pool if you don't know how to swim. All that will happen is that you'll start to drown and never go near water again. First learn the skills you need to survive and then ease yourself in. I recently read a story about a young woman who was terrified of flirting with men. She finally worked up the nerve to give it a shot, but she picked the best-looking man at the bar and approached him while he was standing with a group of his friends. Even for the most accomplished of flirts, this is a difficult scenario to navigate. The poor woman wound up getting mocked by the guy and isn't likely to be flirting with anyone else any time soon. Start small.

Bravery without a strategy isn't going to get you very far. If things don't work out, and you haven't done your homework, you can't blame your luck.

Make a Decision

"Nothing will ever be attempted if all possible objections must first be overcome." – Samuel Johnson

No matter how much homework you do, there will never be a way to know exactly what will happen when you take a risk. None of us can predict the future. At some point, you're going to have to make a decision. Even if option A looks like the best choice, you might very well look back later and wish you'd picked option B. That's the chance you take when you take a chance. But making a decision, any decision, is always better than not deciding at all. Fences aren't a comfortable place to sit.

I was hugely guilty of fence-sitting, myself. It took me about six months to decide whether or not to get divorced. Those were some miserable months for all parties involved. I knew in my gut that separating was the best decision, but I kept letting the fear of making the wrong decision hold me back. What if I never met anyone else and would be alone the rest of my life? What if I hated living by myself? What if in two years I decided I wanted him back? I kept waiting for the moment when I was sure but, not being psychic, I couldn't ever be sure. It took me a lot of time (and tears) to realize I just had to be brave and go after what I wanted.

Making good decisions does involve gathering all the facts that you can, but you can't use fact finding as a way to put off a decision forever. Should I stay with this guy or break up with him? Should I stay in my apartment or move? Should I go to Jamaica or Hawaii? You can waste months, if not years, wavering between choices. There's also the possibility that if you wait too long you won't get to make a decision at all. Your distant behavior causes your boyfriend to break up with you before you figure out want you want, or your lease expires while you were busy fretting about whether to renew it. This is some people's default strategy for decision-making. I think it comes from a desire not to be wrong. They figure that if someone or something else decides for them, then they can't be blamed if it turns out to be a bad decision. But waiting for the luck of the draw gives you the worst possible chance of getting what you want. When you go after something, you might not succeed, but you're a hell of a lot more likely to get it than if you wait for it to land in your lap.

A lot of times we know what we should do, but we're too afraid to do it. As I mentioned, I knew in my gut that I needed to get divorced, but for a long time I was too scared to go through with it. Making a decision like that can feel like jumping off a cliff. Looking down is terrifying, and the longer you stand at the edge, the worse the fear becomes. It can be paralyzing. But the fear is almost always worse than the reality, and the sooner you jump, the sooner you get to see what's in store for you when you land. When I finally went through it, it was nowhere near as bad as I thought it was going to be. As soon as my ex moved out, I was a much happier person. The fear of being alone was much worse than the experience of being alone.

It's in the Stars

"Millionaires don't use Astrology, billionaires do." – J. P. Morgan

What do you do when you have to make a decision, but have no way to decide? What happens when you've done your homework, explored all the logical reasons to pick option A or option B, but you still can't choose? This is when having a superstition – a lucky coin, a favorite number, or an affinity for astrology – can come in handy. Really.

I'll admit it: I love astrology. I read my horoscope every month and keep in mind what my lucky days are supposed to be. You might think it's ridiculous that I plan my life around what the "planetary energy" is like at the time. My husband certainly does. But I believe it makes me extra lucky, and I'll tell you why. In his book, *The Luck Factor*, Max Gunther notes that many rich and famous people have superstitions.[28] He suggests that the reason these arguably silly beliefs lead to so much good luck is that they make us decisive and they make us brave.

First of all, as I mentioned, a superstition can be an excellent way to help you make a difficult decision. There will be times when despite all the research you've done and all of your pro/con lists, you're still not sure which way to go. A superstition can help you get off the fence. You can flip your lucky coin and be done with it. If you're torn between two apartments, and one is on the 7th floor, which happens to be your lucky number, it'll make the decision an easy one.

A superstition can also make you feel more confident in your decisions. If you're thinking about taking a new job and your horoscope says it's a great time to start a new venture, you'll know it's the right decision. As I said in the Belief section, if you believe you're going to win you are more likely to win. If you believe you made the right decision, you'll do everything you can to confirm that belief. You'll see only the good parts of the new job and won't waste time looking over your shoulder at the old one. You'll have a positive attitude and work hard to fit in right away. It will be the right decision because you believed it would be the right decision.

Lastly, a superstition can make you brave because it gives you a *reason* to be brave. When I was single, if my horoscope forecasted a good day for love, it would give me the confidence to call up someone I was interested in. It may or may not have worked out, but I was a hell of a lot more likely to get what I wanted than if I had just sat by the phone. As I've said before, bravery and luck go hand-in-hand. It doesn't matter what motivates you to be brave so long as you are. If having a lucky t-shirt is what it takes, then treasure that t-shirt. When you have a lucky charm, you are the one who makes it lucky.

Love Is Scary

"'Tis better to have loved and lost then never to have loved at all." – Alfred Lord Tennyson

There is a particular kind of bravery required when it comes to matters of the heart. Part of falling in love is risking that someone might not love you back, and part of being in love is managing the fear of losing your love. Few things in life are as terrifying as risking your heart, but nothing can make you feel quite so lucky as being in love.

Love requires a leap of faith, and it comes with no guarantees. Early on in a relationship it's never possible to know how things are going to turn out. You have to be willing to open yourself up, even though it might turn out badly. You can't close yourself off and expect any love to come in. Everyone is nervous when they start dating someone they like, but some are able to label it differently. Some are able to use their beliefs and interpretation skills to their advantage. They believe that things will work out for them, so they have a positive attitude. They feel the same anxieties as everyone else but they think of it as thrilling, invigorating, electrifying. It's hard to be the most charming, engaging version of yourself if you're feeling terrified and don't believe it will work out. All of those anxious vibes you're giving off will more than likely make that fear a reality. When you're out with someone new, focus on enjoying yourself rather than worrying about whether they like you, or where this is going, or whether they're marriage material. And smile a lot.

Once you're in love, you have to manage the fear that something or someone is going to come along and take it away. I would be devastated if I lost Adam. I know that I would be. But I try not to think about it and choose instead to focus on feeling grateful for every day that we have together. Some days it's easier to do that than others, but I always have to make the effort. After all, what's the alternative? It's too easy to let the fear of loss ruin a wonderful relationship. Fear makes people want control. It inspires jealousy and overprotectiveness. It pushes people to monitor their love's every move, email and phone call. And, of course, the more you try to control your love, the more likely you are to push them away.

Fear also drives some people to "test" their love, by behaving like a crazy bitch for example. Consciously or not, they think that if they push their love away or treat them badly, they can see if their love is strong enough to withstand it. This is a very dangerous idea. If it's early on in a relationship and they're not fully in love with you yet, it will send them running for the hills. If they do stay with you, you've planted a seed of doubt in their mind. If you continue the pattern, the seed will keep growing until your love is finally certain you're not the one for them.

It's very hard to be rational about love. The fear of pain and rejection makes us all pretty stupid. Those who are able to overcome this fear will be the most successful in love. As in every other area of life, the more risks you take, the more success you are likely to find. Yes, at least initially, it will probably mean that you'll experience some failures along with the successes. But you have to keep betting on love if you want to win.

You Deserve To Be Happy

"We only become what we are by the radical and deep-seeded refusal of that which others have made of us." – Jean-Paul Sartre

Sometimes in order to make yourself happy you have to do things that hurt the people you love. To me, there is no better example of this than when I got divorced. My ex-husband was devastated. I had promised to love him and be with him forever and I was leaving. My family was devastated. They had come to love my ex as a son and they were losing him from the family. It also meant that I would be alone and they would have to "worry" about me again. Causing the people around me so much pain and suffering was extremely difficult. Leaving my ex felt like the most selfish thing I had ever done. At times the guilt was overwhelming, but I had to remember that eventually everyone would be better off. My ex would be better off with someone who truly loved him, and my family would eventually see how much happier I would be with someone else. I didn't end my marriage to make everyone unhappy. I did it because it was the only way I knew how to make myself happy. And, as I would regularly have to remind myself, I deserve to be happy. Everyone deserves to be happy. There may be times when you are the only one looking out for your best interests, but you have to do it anyway.

When you make a brave decision, you might lose some people from your life. You will find out who your friends really are. A good friend will be there for you even if they may not understand why you are doing what you're doing. Others who you thought were friends might not be so supportive. I was in the unfortunate position of divorcing a man who nearly everyone thought was the nicest guy in the world. I did too when I met him; it just turned out that he wasn't the greatest husband. Having never been married to him, most people couldn't see that. There were those who felt I must be to blame and said some pretty nasty things to me. Some said that I was a horrible person who only thought about herself. Some said that I was going to be alone forever because no one else would want me. Some even told me that I was hard to love. It was very upsetting, to say the least, to face these personal attacks in the midst of my divorce. But it also made it clear who I could count on when the chips were down. I now cherish the friendship of those who stayed with me when I needed them most.

You are the only one who truly knows what will make you happy. Even if it's hard in the short run, if you know what you're doing is right, it will always be worth it. I am now happier than I have ever been. Adam and I have the kind of marriage I had always dreamed of having, and I never would have found him if I hadn't been willing to make the difficult decision. I wouldn't be happy if I didn't think I deserved to be.

Believe in Yourself

"The worst part of success is trying to find someone who is happy for you." – Bette Midler

When you do get up the courage to change your life and go after what you want, you will find that some people aren't as happy about that decision as you are. When you do something bold, there will always be what I like to call "haters." The haters in your life will quickly make themselves known. They can sense when someone is taking a chance and will run right out to tramp down that instinct. As I've said before in this chapter, most people are afraid. Most people aren't brave. So when they see someone else doing something brave, they will project their fear onto you. Because they would never do something new and different, they don't think that anybody else should, either.

Haters have built their lives around the idea that you always have to make the safe, practical, and rational choice. They fear change, and they really, really hate any kind of risk. When you try something new, they will vicariously feel all the fear they would feel if they were in your situation. They will think they are "helping" you by trying to prevent you from doing what you want. Part of the reason some people were so upset when I got divorced was that they were picturing themselves in my position. They were horrified by the idea of having to be single again and start all over on their own. They couldn't see that it was the right decision for me because it wouldn't have been the right decision for them.

To the haters, all risks are too risky. They justify their own reticence to try anything new or do anything different by convincing themselves that it's not worth the risk. To make themselves feel better, they believe risk takers are reckless gamblers who will inevitably regret their decisions. If they were to see someone take a risk and have that risk pay off, it would disrupt their view of the world. If someone took a risk and succeeded, it might mean that they were wrong to have never taken a risk. No one likes to be wrong. Whether or not they would admit this to you or to themselves, they will be rooting for you to fail. And if you do win, they'll think you're just lucky.

They won't give you any credit for having been brave enough to take the risk.

Even if the change you're making is indisputably good, you will likely face pushback. Let's say you have committed to getting healthy and losing fifty pounds. Even though everyone in your life should be supporting you in this goal, there will be those rooting against you. If you succeed, how can they justify not getting healthy? They'll have to feel bad about themselves. They'll have to admit that their own poor health is their own fault. They'll seek to avoid this by sabotaging you in little ways, like bringing you cupcakes or suggesting you see a movie instead of going to the gym. Don't let them win.

It can be hard to go your own way. You might not see many other people on the road you're on. It's a very human trait to seek approval and want to be part of a crowd. But if the crowd you're in wants to hold you back, you might have to find a new crowd. You have to learn to listen to your own voice above all the others. You don't need anyone's permission to go after what you want.

Caveat

Risk/Reward Ratio

Not all risks are created equal, and not all risks are worth taking. The potential payoff should always justify the risk. Big risks can lead to big rewards, but that isn't always the case. If a big risk has a small payoff, it's not worth taking the chance. Always know how much a risk might cost you, and how much you stand to gain.

Test the Waters

You never want to take a big risk when a small risk would work just as well. In many cases it's possible to take a small risk, see how that goes, and then decide if you want to risk more from there. Making too big of a bet upfront is rarely a good idea; you want to see how the cards stack up before putting all of your chips into the pile.

BETH BRUDER

TENET #6: PERSISTENCE

"It is vain to expect our prayers to be heard if we do not strive as well as pray." – Aesop

Most of the time you're not going to find the luck you're looking for on the first day or on the first try. This means, of course, that if you give up looking at the first sign of trouble, you're never going to find luck. Most things in life worth having require time and effort. You have to be willing to invest a lot of both if you want to be lucky. More often than not, persistence is all that separates the victors from the vanquished.

Effort, Outcome, and Motivation

"Great things are not done by impulse, but by a series of small things brought together." – Vincent Van Gogh

What makes many goals so difficult to achieve is the gap that exists between effort and outcome. There is a lag – and often a big one – between the time when you make an effort and the day when you are able to reap the reward. Weight loss is an excellent example. If you have a hundred pounds to lose, it will take a really, really long time to do it. Motivating yourself to go to the gym on any given night can be a challenge when you might have to wait the better part of a year to see the results. It can be difficult to motivate yourself to eat well when any individual meal will hardly make a difference. Time passes one night and one meal at a time. The amount of joy that can be gained from a delicious dinner and an evening watching your favorite TV show can be great, particularly when compared with the slim chance that you might one day be able to reap the reward from the effort of forgoing that pleasure. But if the reward is what you desire, it can only be won by making the right choices and efforts over the course of many days. To become successful, you have to keep going, one day at a time, one step at a time.

People often think that the first step is the hardest, but I don't agree. Personally, I think the hardest step comes somewhere between the starting line and the finish. Whenever you start something new, you're full of energy and enthusiasm and go at it with a gung ho attitude. But pursuing lofty goals requires hard work. Eventually, you will get tired, or bored, or frustrated, or scared. The energy you have at the start is almost never enough to power you to the finish. And so there you are, stranded somewhere between points A and B. It is what you decide to do at this moment that determines the outcome of any venture. At this point, turning back will start to seem like a really good idea. You'll remember how easy and pleasurable your old situation was and conveniently forget the problems you were having. And you look ahead and see *just how much further* you have to go before you reach your goal. This is when I want you to be able to reach inside your pocket and pull out a list of all the reasons why you must reach your goal, no matter what it takes.

Before you make any moves towards accomplishing a goal, make sure you are very clear about why you want what you want – and then write it down. Keep a record of your motivations. Write about how happy you'll be when you do lose the weight, or get your small business going, or finish that screenplay you've been working on. Hopefully you did this when you decided upon your focus, but if not, do it now. Be sure to include on that list all of the reasons why you can't go back. Deal-breakers can be particularly helpful in this regard. A deal-breaker is something that makes it absolutely impossible for you to return to your old ways; it cuts off the option completely. There are pros and cons to every situation, but when you're up against a deal-breaker, you have no choice. Someone who has developed type 2 diabetes can't possibly return to their old eating habits. Someone who has left an abusive relationship can't possibly go back to their partner. For some people, their deal-breaker was a moment when they hit rock bottom, a moment when they could no longer pretend they didn't have a problem. Or perhaps it's simply a realization that you must, must, must pursue your dreams right now and cannot delay a moment longer. Your old life is simply not good enough for you anymore.

Leaving my last job was a difficult decision. I was great at what I did and my employers valued and respected me. I knew how lucky I was to work in such a positive environment. Breaking the news to my boss, who I liked very much, was excruciating. But sticking with my decision during the two weeks before I left, and for months afterwards when I knew they would happily take me back, was much harder. Once I announced I was leaving, all I could think about were the things I would miss and how comfortable it was to be in a secure position with a steady paycheck and good health care benefits. I also realized how much hard work it would take to write a book and how uncertain it was that it would ever succeed. But I had a deal-breaker: I knew, without a shadow of a doubt, that if I didn't write this book I would always regret it. It was the perfect time for my husband and I to take this risk, and I knew that I had to take it, difficult though it might be.

When you're coming up with your own deal-breaker, be honest with yourself. If you are unhappy with your current situation, don't pretend otherwise. Change can be difficult, and you will only be motivated to make that change day after day after day if you are clear about why you *must*. When your old behaviors start to look really good, you have to know why they are no longer an option. When you understand why you must move forward it becomes a lot easier to resist the urge to turn back.

Form a Habit

"All our life, so far as it has definite form, is but a mass of habits." – William James

In recent years there has been a plethora of research on how habits are formed and how they can be changed. Much of this research is nicely summarized in Charles Duhigg's fascinating book, *The Power of Habit*.[29] Given the huge technological advances in the field of neuroscience, scientists have been able to see what happens inside your brain when you're engaging in habitual behavior, i.e. any action that you perform so often that it has become automatic. There are many examples of this sort of behavior, from brushing your teeth in the morning to changing into your pajamas at night. Habits can be good, like going to the gym every day, or they can be bad, like having three doughnuts for breakfast every morning. What all habits have in common, however, is that they have become so routine as to *no longer require your brain to actively think about what you're doing*. The potential value of this information is huge: if you can form good habits that will help you to reach your goals, you won't even have to think about being persistent. It would happen automatically.

As Duhigg describes, all habits consist of three factors: cue, routine, and reward. The cue is what prompts you to begin the routine, the routine itself is the habit, and the reward is what motivates you to do that routine. Stepping into the shower is the cue for you to begin to wash your hair, the action of washing your hair is the routine, and having clean hair will be the reward. Turning on the football game is the cue to reach for a beer, drinking the beer is the routine, and the reward will be a feeling of calm or enjoyment.

In order to create a new habit, then, these three factors must be present. First, decide what new routine you want to perform. Let's say you want to learn a new language. In order to that, you need to come up with a specific routine, such as studying for half an hour every night. Next, you need to find a cue. Maybe you could change the home page of your internet browser to a language learning site. When you got home from work, it would be the first thing you saw on your computer, prompting you to begin the routine. Lastly, and perhaps most importantly, you need to give yourself a reward. In some cases, the feeling of accomplishment can be its own reward. In many others, however, you'll need something more concrete, like having a glass of wine after the half hour is up. Once you've come up with the cue, the routine, and the reward, you'll have to repeat them in succession often enough for your mind to associate the three together. When you see the cue, you'll automatically begin the routine and then receive the reward. You'll know you have succeeded in creating a habit when the cue itself causes you to crave the reward. If seeing the language learning website makes you want a glass of wine, you've done your job.

Many of us also wish to change our current routines. We have a habit that we know is bad, and we need a way to rid ourselves of it. Research suggests that the "golden rule" for doing this is to keep the cue and the reward same, but to change the routine. Let's say you want to stop your habit of eating a cupcake every afternoon. Your first step is to figure out what the cue is. It could be the clock turning to 3:00pm, it could be when you start getting sleepy in the afternoon, or it could be finishing a hated task at work. It's also very important to examine what the reward is. It might seem obvious – cupcakes taste good. But there is likely more to it than that. Maybe you enjoy taking a break. Maybe it's the sugar rush. Maybe you like gossiping with your co-workers on the walk to the bakery. If the afternoon hits and you're tired, or you want an escape from the office, try going out for coffee instead. Or eating some fruit if you're craving sugar. The critical thing is to find a substitute to the original routine that provides you with the same kind of reward. It's much, much harder to break a habit if you don't.

The final ingredient to permanent habit formation and change harkens back to tenet number one: belief. Duhigg explains that the cue, routine, and reward alone are enough to change most routines most of the time, but they tend to break down when an obstacle is encountered. You might have had an easy enough time giving up the cupcakes, but if you faced a crisis at work it might send you right back to the bakery. The key, it seems, is to believe that you can cope with stress without the cupcake. Until you believe that the habit has changed, you'll have a difficult time.

Build Your Discipline

"Any asshole can chase a skirt, art takes discipline." – Charles Bukowski

Research has demonstrated that willpower works much like any other muscle in your body: if you put it under too much strain, it will give out on you. Take a study conducted in 1998 by Baumeister and colleagues in which participants were offered cookies prior to tackling a logic problem.[30] Unbeknownst to the study participants, the puzzle was impossible to complete. The question of interest was how long the participants would struggle with it before giving up. It seems that those who had used their willpower to pass up the cookies gave up a lot more quickly than those who had indulged.

This concept explains nicely why it can be so hard to stick to a strict diet, for example. If you're trying to give up sugar, dairy, and alcohol all at the same time, it's going to be a tough go (as my Canadian husband would say). By the time you've skipped your usual morning latte, and said no to the birthday cake being handed out at the office, your willpower muscles will have been given a workout. If you're going out to dinner with your girlfriends, chances are good you won't have enough willpower strength left to forgo a cocktail.

What is so insidious about this cycle – the biting off more than you can chew and then inevitably failing cycle – is that it undercuts your ability to believe. As I suggested in the previous section, a critical factor in changing your patters is *believing* that you can change your patterns. The more times you fail, the harder it becomes to believe that you'll eventually succeed.

A much better approach is to set small, easily achievable goals. It's much easier to build on small accomplishments over time than to try to tackle a big goal all at once. Big goals can seem almost impossible to achieve at the outset. At times writing this book felt like an endless enterprise. What I found to be critically important was to set smaller goals that would eventually add up to my big goal. I divided the work into chapters. Writing a single chapter felt manageable, and when I would finish one I'd celebrate as though I'd finished the whole book. I felt like I was getting somewhere, which was in stark contrast to how I felt before I broke the book into pieces. Writing one chapter, twelve times, was a lot easier than trying to write the whole book at once.

Luck is an odds game. You increase the odds that you'll win your bet if it's a safe one. The payout might not be huge, but you should be able to win that safe bet over and over again, resulting in bigger and better gains over time. Winning a safe wager many times is a lot more likely to get you what you want than taking one big, risky chance.

Practice, Practice, Practice

"Opportunity is missed by most people because it is dressed in overalls, and looks like work." – Thomas Edison

In his book, *The Outliers*, Malcolm Gladwell made famous the ten thousand hours theory, which states that to be extraordinarily good at something, you have to work at it for ten thousand hours.[31] The theory is meant to debunk the myth that some people are just born with exceptional talent and would have succeeded whether they worked at it or not. Talent plays some part in it, but there a lot of people with some talent for hockey. What separates the Wayne Gretzky's from those who never make it to the NHL? The answer, it seems, is a constant, unrelenting drive to become better at your craft. Gladwell cites a study conducted in the early 1990's at Berlin's Academy of Music, where the researchers asked professors to divide the violin students into three groups: (1) The stars, those with the potential to become world-class soloists; (2) Good violinists, who were talented but did not have quite as much potential; and (3) The not-very-good, who were unlikely to make it professionally.[32] As it turns out, what separated the groups was not their innate talent, but the number of hours they had spent practicing the violin. By the age of 20, the top performers had totaled 10,000 hours of practice, while the "good" group had practiced about 8,000 hours, and the "not very good" only about 4,000 hours. The researchers did not find a single student who reached the "star" group with fewer than 10,000 hours of practice, nor did they find anyone who had practiced that much and had not achieved the elite level. The same trend is seen among experts in just about every field. Apparently hard work really does pay off.

Even if you're not training to be a concert violinist, practice is still vitally important. Talented people are expected to perform at their best when it counts the most. Star athletes have to come up with the big hit or big goal in the important games, musicians have to sound their best at big concerts, and at one time or another we will all be called upon perform under pressure. A lot of research has been done on how people behave in front of an audience.[33] In some cases, people flourish, performing better than they would have if no one was watching. In other cases, they flounder, making more mistakes than they would on their own. What makes the difference between whether you will perform better or worse in the critical moments is how comfortable you are with the task at hand. There is an old military adage that states: "We do not rise to the occasion, but rather fall back to our level of training." If you are well practiced at a task, having others around will serve to push you to perform at a high level. But if the task is in any way novel or uncomfortable, having an audience will only make things worse.

Further, practice is a tool that can be used in many circumstances. We tend to think of practice as related to things like an instrument or a sport, but one can practice just about anything. Practice is a way to become comfortable with anything that might presently make you uncomfortable. You can practice public speaking. You can practice flirting or meeting new people. You can even practice dating. By definition, dating is something you do in front of an audience, and if you're not comfortable with it, you aren't very likely to make it to a second date. Internet dating is a great way to become comfortable with being on a date. Some people will go on interviews for jobs they don't want as practice before interviewing for a job they desperately want. If you've never been on a job interview, there is no way you'll perform as well as if you've been on twenty. Getting comfortable with social and professional situations that make you uneasy is the best way to ensure you'll be on the top of your game when it counts.

Take a Chance (and Another, and Another, and Another)

In his book, *The Drunkard's Walk*, Leonard Mlodinow discusses the role played by randomness in every venture.[34] Environmental factors beyond your control can, and often do, determine whether you win or lose. For this reason, Mlodinow stresses the need to keep on taking chances. While any one chance might not pay off, if you keep trying, over and over again, eventually you might find what you're looking for. He uses the experiences of John Grisham and J.K. Rowling to illustrate his point. These writers are among the most famous and best-selling of all time. Their books are almost universally adored. And yet it took each of them years of trying before they finally became successful. John Grisham's *A Time to Kill* was rejected by 28 publishers before he saw his book in print. Even then, it wasn't until after publishing a second book, *The Firm*, that sales took off. J.K. Rowling was rejected by the first 12 publishers she submitted her book to. When her book was eventually published, only 1,000 copies were printed and she was advised to get a day job. Seven years later, *Forbes* named Rowling the first writer to become a billionaire.[35] As Mlodinow puts it, "That's why successful people in every field are almost universally members of a certain set – the set of people who don't give up."

Let's say that going after what you want is like rolling a pair of dice. Let's say that "success" is represented by rolling two sixes. The odds that you'll succeed on any individual roll are slim (1 in 36, to be exact). Yet the odds are excellent that you'll succeed if you keep rolling over and over again. If you roll those dice 36 times, you're almost certain to get what you want. But rolling dice is easy. It doesn't take any effort and you can do it repeatedly in quick succession. The same cannot be said for most things. Each chance you take will likely require a lot of effort. It will be difficult. If, after all that work, you don't succeed, it can be challenging to motivate yourself to try again. But you have to, and the odds only begin to work in your favor when you keep trying. The more chances you take, the more chances you give yourself to win, and odds are you'll need to take a lot of chances.

Don't Look Down

Our doubts are traitors and make us lose the good we oft might win." – William Shakespeare

Jonathan Tropper's novel, *The Book of Joe*, is one of my favorites.[36] At one point in the story a main character talks about faith, using the old Road Runner cartoons as a metaphor. In them, Wile E. Coyote would frequently run off a cliff, and keep running until he looked down and saw there was no road beneath his feet, at which point he would start to fall. The character poses the question, "What would have happened if he never looked down?" He goes on to say that he thinks we're all like this – we start off in the direction of something we want, but as soon as we notice we're not on solid ground, we panic and try to run back to where we started. For both us and the Coyote, if we could just keep looking straight ahead, we could get to where we want to go.

Much of persistence is about keeping the faith. When we stumble, it's often not because we stop wanting what we want, but because we stop believing it's possible to get. And as I hope I conveyed in the Belief section, you can only achieve what you believe you can achieve. When you don't think something is possible, you won't give it your best effort. You start to ask, "What's the point?" And soon enough what you want will have slipped out of reach and you'll have proven yourself right.

Everyone has moments of doubt. Everyone has days where the finish line seems so far away that it's impossible to believe they'll ever get there. There are times when you will feel you know exactly what you're doing and have all the faith in the world in your ability. And then there will be days when you doubt yourself, especially if things aren't turning out the way you'd planned. Know that this is normal. Know that this is part of the process. And then just keep going.

Sometimes I think the world tests our faith on purpose. It serves as a screening process. We don't tend to value things we come by too easily. The universe uses it as a way to sort those who are really committed to something from those who aren't. How much do you really want what you want? You have to be prepared to answer that question because it's very likely to be asked.

Caveat

As important as it is to be persistent, there are a number of caveats. So many, in fact, that much of the next chapter is devoted to exploring them.

TENET #7: FEXIBILITY

"Like all weak men he laid an exaggerated stress on not changing one's mind." – W. Somerset Maugham

When most people think about getting lucky, they focus on good luck: lucky breaks, happy coincidences, winning big, et cetera. But a huge determinant of how lucky any person will be in their life is how they manage bad luck. Bad luck lands on everyone's doorstep from time to time. Not everything you try will work out and not every gamble will pay off. Flexibility is critical when handling the fallout. In our culture, flexibility tends to get a bad name. We celebrate those who remain firm in their convictions and "stick to their guns." But when bad luck comes barreling down towards you, you need to be nimble enough to jump out of its way to escape the worst of its damage. You might not be able to prevent bad luck, but you can prevent bad luck from turning into worse luck.

If the Ship is Sinking, Jump.

"Fanaticism consists in redoubling your effort when you have forgotten your aim." – George Santayana

Having just read a chapter on the importance of persistence, you might be wondering why I'm telling you to abandon ship. Persistence is a virtue, but only to a point. Persistence is a virtue when you stay with a course of action when there is *still the possibility that you can succeed*. Persistence becomes a vice when the chances of success are slim to none and you keep on persisting anyway. Flexibility is about knowing the difference and acting accordingly.

Evaluate As You Go Along

"It's astonishing in this world how things don't turn out at all the way you expect them to." – Agatha Christie

Every time you take a risk, there is always the chance that things aren't going to work out. You can't know at the outset which way things are going to go. Say to yourself: "Let's see what happens. If it's not working out, I'll cut my losses and try something else." Instead, too many people say, "I've made a decision, and so now I've got to live with it no matter what." A small failure can become a big one if you're not willing to change course. Let's say you take a new job and quickly discover it's not what you thought it would be and you know you won't be happy there. Someone who has allowed for this possibility would immediately send out some resumes, call their contacts in the industry, or even try to get their old job back. They'll spend a few weeks or months in the position, and then their ship will be righted and their lives back on course. But someone who feels they must stick with the decision might waste years toiling each day at a place they don't want to be. And the longer they stay, the harder it is to leave. Suddenly they're eligible for a pension and a bonus. Can't leave now, can they? It's much easier to abandon a bad situation early on. The longer you stay with it, the more entangled you will become.

Make a Mistake

It seems so obvious – if something isn't working, try something new. But this is very difficult for many people, for one simple reason: *changing your mind means admitting you were wrong*. Quitting a job you just started means admitting that taking it was a bad idea. Selling a losing stock means admitting that buying it was the wrong decision. Ending a relationship means admitting that you picked the wrong person. No one likes being wrong. It's embarrassing, it might damage your reputation, and you might anger or disappoint some people. Admitting a mistake can be painful in the moment and can have some serious short term consequences. But it's a hell of a lot better than remaining in a bad situation because you're not brave enough to be wrong. Everyone makes mistakes occasionally. Not being able to admit it means resigning yourself to a life full of mistakes you're not willing to rectify.

Stop Investing

What if you moved across the country to take that new job? What if you spent most of your savings on your small business? What if you've spent years trying to succeed as an actor? The more time, energy, and money you have invested in a venture, the more difficult it becomes to leave. In fact, research has demonstrated that most people would much rather continue to invest in a losing proposition with a very slight chance of success than stop investing and guarantee their failure. As long as you're still investing, you're keeping the hope alive that some miracle might come along and save the day. Logically, it makes no sense. A reasonable person *should* take a certain loss of $5,000 over a very, very likely loss of $10,000, but few are able to do so in the heat of the moment.

Most failing situations don't come to an abrupt end, but gradually decline over time. There might never come a time when it's 100% clear that it won't work out. There are those who are able to see the way things are heading early on and are able to pull out before all is lost. And then there are those who will keep clinging to the sinking ship until they drown. Be one of the former. When there is no longer a realistic chance of success, stop investing.

Allow For Change

Just because something has worked in the past, it does not mean it will work in the future. A lot of people get stuck on a losing course of action because the course used to be a winning one. Think of it like investing in VHS tapes. At one point in the 1980s that would have been a great idea. But once DVDs were introduced in the 1990s, investing in VHS tapes would have been a *very bad idea*. People are always changing. The world around us is always changing. It can be difficult to walk away from something that has brought you success in the past, but you must evaluate whether something is working *today*. Is there a good possibility that things might turn around? Or are you just feeling nostalgic for good times gone by? Make sure you know the difference.

I see this happen most often in relationships. Once you've loved someone, either romantically or platonically, it becomes very hard to see them as they are now and not as they were. It's difficult to understand how something that was once so wonderful could go wrong. It can take time for problems to emerge in a relationship. Or one or both of you could simply have changed. Relationships aren't all designed to last forever. Some people will be important to us in one phase of our lives but no longer fit later on. Hanging on to a relationship that has run its course will only lead to prolonged pain and heartbreak.

Don't Expect Imperfection

Nothing is perfect. People say this a lot when they're busy stagnating in a bad situation. They tell themselves that no matter what job they have they would be bored, so they might as well stay at the one they have. No relationship is ever perfect, so they might as well stick with the one they've got. I heard this "advice" a lot when I was getting divorced – every relationship will have problems, so why bother getting divorced? They said that my desire for a more satisfying relationship was unrealistic. "Why should a new relationship be any different? *You're* still the same person. *You* will still have the same issues." If you're getting divorced because you are an alcoholic, or you have a gambling addiction, or you are a chronic liar, then yes, you will probably have the same problems in your next relationship. But if you're simply unhappy with your spouse, and you cannot see any way to salvage the situation, it is wiser to move on. It is true that nothing will ever be perfect, but that's not a good enough reason to settle for something that you tolerate rather than enjoy. There is a lot of room for improvement between "okay" and "perfect."

A Flexible Approach

"The measure of intelligence is the ability to change." – Albert Einstein

"There's more than one way to skin a cat." A bit gruesome maybe, but this common saying makes a good point: there is always more than one way to accomplish your goal. Often when people find their focus and bravely set off towards their desired destination, they also commit themselves to a particular course of action. Let's say you want to lose fifty pounds. In order to do that you've committed to going to the gym five days a week and eating only 1,200 calories a day. But after a few days you're exhausted and starving. Some might give up entirely and head straight to the closest bakery. Others, though not many I imagine, trudge on, and stay miserable. Isn't there a third option? Why not say to yourself, "This isn't working. What else can I try?" Selecting a different route from A to B doesn't mean you'll never get to B. In fact, if you see the route you're on isn't getting you very far, find a better way. Finding a better way will save you a lot of time and frustration.

Approach your goals with flexibility. You can know where you want to go, and can have some idea of how you want to get there, but be willing learn and change as you go. When you're writing a paper or a book or a speech, you start with an outline. You have a general idea of what you want to say and the order you want to say it in, but when you start doing some research, you might come across something great that doesn't fit neatly into your outline. Don't be so married to what your idea was at the outset that you're unwilling to modify it along the way.

Further, it's always a good idea to build flexibility into any plan. Give yourself some options. Think of it like planning a vacation. You can plan out everything in advance – every hotel room, every activity, and every town you want to explore. Or you can get to your destination and decide if you like your hotel or you want to stay somewhere else. Or talk to some locals and figure out what's worth seeing. There's nothing wrong with planning, so long as your plan is flexible.

Lastly, as I've said, there are a lot of ways to get from A to B. But what if on the way to B, you discover you'd really rather go to C? Sometimes the very actions we take to get us what we want lead us to realize we don't want it after all. When you begin medical school, you start spending lots of time in hospitals around sick, injured, and dying people. You're busy becoming a doctor – what you thought you wanted – when it becomes clear to you that you don't like being around sick, injured, and dying people. You absolutely still *can* become a doctor, but it's probably a better idea pursue a different career. There's nothing wrong with deciding on a new destination. At the end of the day, everyone's goal is to be happy. It doesn't matter how you get there as long as you do.

Be Prepared

Speaking of planning, it's best to be prepared for anything. Before beginning any venture, try to determine all possible outcomes and consider how you might manage each one. I have a good friend who is the principal of a charter school. Pretty much everything she does could have a myriad of outcomes, and it's her job to be prepared for them. Some of her teachers think she's paranoid, but when several kids showed up to the SAT without their graphing calculators, who do you think had spares to lend them? She's great at her job because she's the one who makes sure she has a plan for anything that could go wrong. You always want to go into a venture believing that things will go well and no difficulties will arise, but that's not an excuse to be unprepared. If you're prepared you don't have waste time worrying that there might be a problem; you know that you'll be fine if there is so you can stay focused on achieving your goal.

Unfortunately, however, no matter how prepared you are, there is always the possibility that things won't work out in your favor. Every venture you undertake might succeed or it might fail. Knowing this, it's critical to have a plan in place for what you will do if it fails. Failure is always difficult to cope with, but if you've planned for that possibility, you can make things a lot easier on yourself. For instance, say what you will about pre-nuptial agreements, but there have been many couples who were happy they had them. It is a lot easier to have a calm, rational discussion about the equitable division of assets before you get married – and are madly in love – than when you're in the midst of a divorce and probably don't like one another very much. No one wants to get divorced, but the experience of it can be much improved with some preparation.

If you can, another good idea is to hold off on committing until you know if your plan will succeed. A friend of mine is moving with his wife and child to Colorado. They're attracted to the school districts and property values and think it'll be a great place to raise a family. I wish them the best of luck, but it's far from certain that things work out as well as they hope. They don't know anyone in Colorado and neither of them has ever lived outside of the East Coast. Why not build an escape clause into the plan? Why not rent out their current place instead of selling it? Why not rent in Colorado until they're sure they want to stay? Yes, if all goes according to plan, they might be creating some extra work for themselves down the road. But if things don't go the way they want, they'll be glad to have an easy out.

Look for Detours

"There are those who would misteach us that to stick in a rut is consistency – and a virtue, and that to climb out of the rut is inconsistency – and a vice." – Mark Twain

Something doesn't have to be going wrong in your life for you to decide to change directions. Sometimes the opportunities that fall into your lap are the best possible kind of luck. In order to benefit from them, however, you have to be willing to seize them.

Let's say you're moving right along in your plan – work is going great, and you know you're going to get a promotion any day now. But then one day a friend you haven't talked to in years calls you up with an amazing opportunity. She's starting a small business and it's exactly the kind of thing you'd love to do.

It might be a little risky, but she has a solid business plan and you know you'll be able to help out her company. What do you do? There are a lot of people that will look at all that they've built up in their present job and say, "Well, I can't abandon all of this work that I've done. I have to wait around to see it pay off." But pay off with what exactly? More of the same? If it's not your dream job, it probably isn't worth it. You can feel safe and reasonably content, but you probably won't be happy. You might be comfortable financially, but you'll never be rich. Meanwhile, this other opportunity provides you with a chance to be fantastically happy and wealthier than you could have imagined. The only catch, of course, is that it's not a *certainty*. There are those that are willing to seize opportunities when they come along, scary thought they might be, and then there are those that won't and will stay on the path of least resistance. But I think we all know who is going to be "luckier" in their lives. Let's say persons A and B were both offered the same opportunity. They could have had the same luck. But only one of them takes the chance, and only one of them is going to be rich, powerful and fulfilled five years from now. Lucky for her, right?

As I discussed in Bravery, go ahead and evaluate the worst-case scenario. If you're doing well at your job but you have the chance to try something new, it's always possible that your old company would be willing to take you back if things go wrong. I know when I left my last job, they said they'd be happy to have me back someday. If you don't burn your bridges there's no reason you can't head right back to the road you were on if the venture goes awry. The things is, in my experience, once you get off the road you're on you realize how glad you are to be off it. When you see how good a different kind of life can be, you'll wonder why you didn't try it sooner.

Max Gunther, author of the book *The Luck Factor*, was a Princeton grad and on the eve of his 25-year reunion took it upon himself to survey his classmates about how happy they were.[37] The ones who were the happiest, and most successful, and who felt the luckiest, were the ones who took the most risks. A survey question asked how many different companies they had worked for and/or how many different ventures they had started. The majority of those with six or more jobs or ventures were very satisfied with their lives. Of those who only had one job or started only one venture, many were disappointed with how their lives had turned out. Security is overrated.

Often the problem is that people don't even see the opportunities that are offered to them. Let's say your old friend calls you and you never bother to call her back. You're not looking to try something new, and so you never bother to hear her out. You're not on the lookout for opportunities, so you don't even know that one has passed you by. You have to keep your head up. Don't be so sure that you know the best way your life can go right now. Always be willing to learn about new things that come your way. Some of the best things that will happen to you are those that you never could have anticipated.

Even slight detours can be helpful. You might not be able to see any way that an opportunity could benefit you, but you never do know. Embrace everything that comes your way unless you have a compelling reason not to. If your friend asks you to join a dodge ball team, say yes. The universe works in mysterious ways. Maybe some guy on that dodge ball team is going to be your future husband. I've seen it happen. Seriously. Dodge ball. All I'm saying is that you never know. At worst, you'll become a more interesting person because of it.

Flexible Relationships

"That which yields is not always weak." – Jacqueline Carey,
Kushiel's Dart

I often find that the people who are least happy in their relationships are those that have decided that they will never leave, no matter what. So much of that is admirable; it's important to take your commitments seriously. I would just like to point out the subtle difference between doing everything you can to keep your commitment, and blindly keeping your commitment regardless of the circumstance. Good relationships require a lot of maintenance; if you're certain your relationship will last, no matter what, what incentive do you have to work on maintaining it? For example, if I know for sure that my husband will never leave me, I don't have to make an effort to be attractive, or go out of my way to treat him well, or be financially responsible. You give yourself the option of taking the relationship for granted. Those of us that allow for the possibility that our spouse might leave us go the extra mile to ensure their continuing happiness. I tell Adam all the time that I will never leave him, but I know he interprets it the way it is intended – not that I would never leave no matter what, but that I would never leave without doing everything I could to fix whatever was wrong.

Flexibility is not about creating uncertainty, and I most certainly don't advise threatening to leave your partner if he forgets to take the garbage out one night. It's about having an expectation of being treated well and not being willing to tolerate less. Many people say that any relationship can be fixed if you're willing to work at it. I absolutely agree with this. What is critical to that equation, however, is the willingness of both parties to do the work. If your partner believes you will never leave him or her, they might not feel motivated to make the effort having a good relationship requires. I had this problem in my first marriage. My ex-husband blithely assumed that since we were married, I wasn't going anywhere. I couldn't get him to listen to me. When I complained about how unhappy I was, he ignored me. Our relationship wasn't his priority. It wasn't until I wanted a divorce that he realized there was a problem. Suddenly he was willing to change, but by then it was too late.

Lucky Failure

"But plans are one thing and fate another. When they coincide, success results. Yet success musn't be considered the absolute. It is questionable, for that matter, whether success is an adequate response to life. Success can eliminate as many options as failure." – Tom Robbins, Even Cowgirls Get the Blues

Whenever something goes wrong in my own life I think back to this line from *Even Cowgirls Get the Blues*: "Success can eliminate as many options as failure."[38] We don't often think in these terms, but it is so very true: When we get what we want, there are a lot of other opportunities we're cutting ourselves off from. Maybe we needed to fail at that venture to leave us free to pursue another, better opportunity. It sucks not to get what you want. But how many times have you not succeeded at something, only to later be glad that you didn't? That is, "If I had gotten what I had wanted then, this better thing never would have happened."

I've had this experience many times in my own life, and I'm always comforted by it in my moments of disappointment.

My first job out of college was a miserable ordeal. I graduated at a time when jobs weren't exactly plentiful, especially in marketing, the industry I hoped to get into. Through a friend of the family, I managed to find an entry-level job in advertising. I hadn't really wanted to go into advertising, but at that point I had to take what I could get. This job was a comedy of errors right from the start. Try as I might, I couldn't seem to do anything right. I worked for a woman who wanted me to be able to read her mind. I remember this one (in retrospect, hilarious) conversation I had with her, where I pleaded with her to tell me what she wanted me to do. She kept insisting that I should just *know* what to do and wouldn't elaborate despite my many protestations that I hadn't a clue what she was talking about. I was fired six months later. I was crushed at the time. I had gotten fired from my first full-time job. But it was far and away the best thing that could have happened. Who knows how many years I would have wasted in an industry I didn't want to be in if I had been successful in that position?

Another experience I've had that I know many can commiserate with is getting dumped by the guy I thought I wanted. About a year before I met Adam, I had a brief but intense love affair with a man named Carlos, who I met on vacation in Mexico. We did the long distance thing for a while. I went back to Mexico for a week, and we spent four days together in Las Vegas. Little did I know that when I said good-bye to Carlos in Vegas I would never see or hear from him again. I didn't get so much as a "thanks for the memories" e-mail, and this was from a man who had repeatedly told me he loved me. I suppose it's possible he was abducted by aliens, but I think it's more likely he met a nice Mexican girl. I was devastated at the time, yet I am now beside myself with glee that I didn't run off to Mexico to marry Carlos. I am much, much happier with Adam than I ever could have been with Carlos, and I never would have met Adam if I had gotten what I wanted. It would have helped if I'd known when Carlos ditched me that something better was on the horizon. And that's the trick – *you have to know that something better is on the horizon*. Have faith that it's coming and any disappointments will be a lot easier to stomach.

Cruel to be Kind

"Necessity does the work of courage." – George Elliot

There are times when pain can be your friend. Pain is the universe's U-turn sign. It sends louder and louder signals until you're ready to heed them and make a change.

Sometimes we want the wrong thing. In the examples I just gave, the universe reached in with a big stop sign. Whether or not I kept wanting what I wanted, I couldn't have it. The game was over. But there are times when it looks like we can still have what we want. There are times when we can keep on chasing after the wrong guy or keep working away at the wrong job. In these instances the universe will not always send the clear signal of a total rejection or failure. Sometimes you're going to have to decide for yourself that you're going the wrong way. Usually what happens is it starts to hurt. You're upset, you're unhappy, the situation is unpleasant. And then things get worse and worse and worse. If you wait long enough, you might be forcibly removed from the situation. But the sooner you see the signs, the less pain you'll have to endure. It's always more pleasant to extricate yourself.

Back when I worked in advertising, I should have seen

the writing on the wall right away, but I didn't. There were plenty of signs. Sometimes I've found that when I'm in a bad situation, signs come in the form of crazy coincidences. For example, there was one night that I needed to send out a very important FedEx. The guy absolutely had to have it the next morning. The last FedEx pickup was at 7pm. Every single night I worked there, the FedEx guy came by at 7pm. I left at 6pm with all the confidence in the world that the package would be safely on its way. But when I got to work the next morning, it was still there. A crazy coincidence, something that was totally out of my control, and yet it still made me look completely incompetent. Even worse? That same morning, they decided to send me on a plane to Boston to hand-deliver this package. Okay, no problem, I'll go. I was in a huge rush. I didn't have any cash, so my first stop was the bank. Only then did I discover that my ATM card had expired *that day*. With no alternative, I had to go back to the office to get cash from my boss, who now thought I was really, really incompetent. The FedEx no-show and the ATM card expiration – things that on any other day wouldn't have caused a big problem – conspired to make me look like a blithering idiot. Later on in life I learned to recognize these signs for what they were – clear indicators to get the hell out of dodge. Back then I just cursed my bad luck and tried not to let them see my cry.

If you're trying too hard to force something, it probably means it wasn't meant to be. The universe will help you if you're moving in the right direction. But it will throw up bigger and bigger roadblocks if you aren't. The universe doesn't want to see you in pain. In fact, the universe sends you pain because it so badly wants to see you be happy. Sometimes if it doesn't hurt enough, you won't do anything about it. If something is only tolerably unpleasant you might not be motivated enough to make a major life change. This is why in many cases people have to hit "rock bottom" before they are able to turn things around. They can know for years that they need to lose weight or stop drinking or dump their crazy girlfriend, but it's only when something catastrophically bad happens that they are able to do something about it. When it hurts so bad that you can't stand it, you'll try something new. At that point, you have no choice. Try to remember this if there is anything in your life now that makes you completely miserable. Be grateful for it because misery is a hell of a lot more motivating than mild unpleasantness. If it doesn't hurt enough it's too easy to get stuck in a bad situation.

Live and Learn

"Inside of a ring or out, ain't nothing wrong with going down. It's staying down that's wrong." – Muhammad Ali

People are always saying how failure is such a great thing because we can learn from it. It's provided you with valuable information about what isn't working, so you can revise the plan and do better in the future. True enough, if difficult to stomach. If you're going to fail, at least learn something from it. I know it's hard. Been there and done that. Do your best to see it for what it is – something that can show you how not to fail next time. They say that Thomas Edison tried 10,000 different (failed) versions of the light bulb before he found one that worked. At least you're not Thomas Edison.

When you're learning from failure, it's critical that you learn the right lessons. When a relationship goes wrong, learn about what you did to contribute to the problems, learn about what you want in a future mate, and learn what works for you and what doesn't. But do not, under any circumstances "learn" that you should never fall in love again because it hurts too much. Do not "learn" that all men (or women) are evil and can't be trusted. I personally think having some failed relationships is an incredibly valuable experience. My marriage with Adam is so great partly because I made all the mistakes I was going to make in my first marriage. I made an effort to learn how to be a better wife after that experience and it's paid off.

The worst lesson you can learn from failure is "this will never work." Just because it didn't work this time, or last time, or even the time before that, does not mean that it never will. It never will if you're doing the exact same thing over and over and expecting a different result. But if you can honestly appraise the situation and see where you might be going wrong – and *do it differently the next time* – there's no reason to believe you can't succeed.

It's also important to realize that just because something didn't work out, it doesn't mean that it was a bad decision. We all make the best decisions we can at the time, with what information we have. It might have been a wonderful decision, and you merely encountered some bad luck. Resist the urge to evaluate the merit of a decision or a strategy based solely on the outcome. Of course you should look to see what you could have done better, but also look for factors that were totally beyond your control. If the pool party you threw was a bust because it rained that day, it's hardly an indicator of your party-planning prowess.

Lastly, don't let the way things end color your perception of the whole experience. Having something not work out doesn't mean that it wasn't worthwhile. We learn from everything, and often we learn more from our mistakes than from our triumphs.

Caveat

Don't Take Your Commitments Lightly

If you've committed to something or someone, do not leave at the first sign of trouble. Work diligently to fix any situation or relationship before moving on. You are likely to regret it if you don't. If you do everything you can to remedy a situation and it still doesn't improve, at least you will have known that you tried. You won't look back and wonder what might have been.

Don't Use "Staying Flexible" As A Reason not to Commit to Anything

There is nothing wrong with commitment. Commitment to things and ideas and people is a wonderful thing, and is the best way to harness the power of your focus. You must commit to be successful at anything. But that doesn't mean you have to commit right away, and it doesn't mean that you can't have a contingency plan.

TENET #8: RESPONSIBILITY

"Champions take responsibility. When the ball is coming over the net, you can be sure I want the ball." – Billie Jean King

Responsibility is such a loaded word. It immediately calls to mind all kinds of things we don't like doing but know we have to do. Laundry. Grocery shopping. Going to the gym. Yet there is so much good inside a word with such negative connotations. To me, responsibility means power. If I'm responsible for something, I have the power to do with it whatever I like. It can be good, it can be bad, but it's all up to me. When you're responsible for your life you have the power to make anything happen. If things are bad, you can fix them, and if things are great, you can keep them going. When you take responsibility, you get power.

On the face of it, luck and responsibility don't seem like concepts that should go together. In some ways they are polar opposites. Saying that someone is lucky implies that they weren't responsible for their good fortune. And then there are those that feel that if they work hard enough they don't need luck. The most successful among us are both lucky and responsible. I believe that when you take responsibility for your own happiness and well-being, you're more likely to come across some good luck. And I don't think good luck can take you very far if you're not willing to be responsible for your success. Luck and responsibility are like the perfect kind of couple – each brings out the best in the other.

Make Your Own Luck

"They always say time changes things, but you actually have to change them yourself." – Andy Warhol

If you were waiting for me to tell you how to be lucky without having to do anything for yourself, I'm afraid you're going to be disappointed. In some ways I think luck is like taking a taxi. You're not going to hail a taxi while you're sitting at home. Luck is something you have to go out and get. Once you leave home, you can't control whether or not a cab is going to come your way. Sometimes you'll get lucky right away, and sometimes you'll have to wait a long time. But you can pick a corner where cabs are more likely to drive by. There are always things you can do to position yourself to "catch" some good luck. And while you're waiting for a cab, you can start walking in the right direction. A taxi ride is a short cut. Luck is a shortcut. You can still get where you're going on your own two feet, but it'll take a lot longer and require a lot more energy without a little luck.

It is true that people who were born into privilege will have an easier time becoming successful in life. They have a built-in shortcut. It can be frustrating to look at someone who has a fleet of taxis at their disposal and wonder how you're going to compete. It will be a lot more difficult for you. But "difficult" does not mean "impossible." Get over it. If you're not willing to work for it, you can't want what you think you want very much. It would be like stepping outside your apartment and thinking, "I'll only go to this party if I find a cab right away." You can't pick a goal that's like a party you're not that into. If you want to succeed, your goal has to be like a party in Connecticut that you're going to attend even if you have to take three trains and a bus to get there.

Years ago, I read a horoscope written by my favorite astrologer, Jonathan Cainer, which perfectly illustrates my feelings on the issue:

> "Imagine you are a guardian angel. You are busily wandering the world invisibly, looking for struggling souls to protect. Your team of ethereal assistants is short-staffed – several are attending a harp-playing workshop over on Cloud Nine. Down below, you see two people. One is fed up, but doing nothing much about it. The other is effectively putting up a sign. 'I'm doing all I can. I'm willing to do whatever it takes. One little lightning bolt of luck is all I need.' Which one would you rush to rescue?"[39]

Perhaps there aren't guardian angels that only hand out favors to those who deserve them, but I'm still a believer that the best luck comes for those who are looking for it – and who are working for it. Take an honest assessment of your life right now. Are you waiting for good luck to come your way, or are you out there doing everything you possibly can to move towards your goals? Because if you're not, you can't blame your circumstances on your luck.

Ask For Help

"I get by with a little help from my friends." – John Lennon

"Make your own luck" does not mean "Do it all on your own." Taking responsibility does not mean that you can't accept assistance. In fact, asking for help is critical to success. Having someone help you when you're starting out towards your goal can be the most effective way to get where you're going. There is no point in struggling unnecessarily. There is no point in duplicating effort if someone has already learned the lessons you're trying to learn. Getting there on your own when someone is willing to give you a ride is a waste of effort. Sure, there will be times when you need to learn the lessons yourself. It's okay to forgo a ride if you need to learn the route. But that doesn't mean you can't ask for directions, and if it isn't critical to learn how to get their on your own, accept the ride. Remember: work smart, not hard. Keep the ultimate goal in mind. Taking a longer, harder road is not a wise choice if the longer, harder road has no added benefit. It may feel like cheating to take a shortcut. Earlier in the chapter I suggested that luck is a shortcut. More often than not, a lucky break is a way to bypass a slower, more arduous path. This is what you are looking for. This is what you want. In our culture, we have a tendency to overvalue "doing it all on your own." If two people go after the exact same thing, but one person works harder to get it, is it any more valuable? No, the luckier person is the one who had the easier time of it. (Provided, of course, that the shortcut is a legal and ethical one.)

Asking for help and taking responsibility are not

mutually exclusive. The key distinction is the locus of control. You can maintain control even if you ask for help. If you're looking for a job and a family member offers to get you an interview at their company, it's okay to say yes. You are still the one who took charge of the job search. You are still the one who is going to have to make a good impression during the interview. You are still the one who is going to have to perform well if you get the job. You don't have to think less of yourself for accepting a job you know you couldn't have gotten on your own. Not taking responsibility would be saying, "I will only look for a job if I have a connection and it will be easy." When you let people know what you're looking for and it yields a positive result, you deserve credit for putting yourself out there. Don't discount a lucky opportunity because it looks like help.

Help doesn't have to be financial or a professional connection, it can come in the form of advice. You don't have to reinvent the wheel, as they say. My former workplace was a very collaborative environment. When I was asked to do a project, chances were good that someone else in my department had already done something similar. It would have been a waste of my time to redo something that had already been done. Asking for help made me better at my job because it made me more efficient. Further, never discount the possibility that someone else's idea could be better than your own. If someone has more expertise in an area than you do, go to them for advice. In my office we all "specialized" in one area or another. If someone was the go-to person on a particular topic, it would have been irresponsible not to ask for their opinion. There is nothing embarrassing about asking for help. If you try to accomplish a goal without input or assistance it will take you a long, long time to achieve it – if you manage to achieve it at all.

A good way to become comfortable with accepting help is to ensure that you return the favor one day, either by helping out the person who helped you, or by providing the same opportunity to someone else down the road. Help can be contagious and it can lead to a lot of good luck.

Make Your Own Love

"Much more genius is needed to make love than to command armies." – Ninon de L'Enclos

Many people have a very romantic notion of love. They believe that one day they'll meet The One and everything will fall perfectly into place and they'll live happily ever after. It will be easy and magical and require absolutely no effort on their part. Mr. or Ms. Right will make it immediately obvious that they're madly in love and woo them passionately from their first glance until their dying breath.

The romantics out there see love as something that happens to you, something that you have no control over. Being swept off your feet is a lovely notion, except that it implies that someone else is going to have to do the sweeping. Is it really fair to expect your potential mate to be in charge of all the romance? Take a moment to think about how selfish an idea that is: "I'm not willing to look for someone, but I expect to be found. I'm not willing to expose myself to ridicule and rejection, but I expect someone else to. I'm not willing to do any seducing, but I expect to be seduced." Everyone wants to be romanced. Romance is – or should be – a give and take. Rejection isn't fun for anyone. If you're not willing to put yourself out on a limb, you can't expect anyone else to, either. Think about how much more likely you are to find a date if you're willing to ask for one. Even if you're not willing to ask, think about how much more likely you are to be asked if the person doing the asking is sure you'll say yes.

Women in particular fall prey to the notion that love will come to them and feel they need only to look pretty and wait patiently in their ivory tower. As it happens, research has shown that women initiate two-thirds of all romantic encounters. In her book, *How to Make Anyone Fall in Love with You*, Leil Lowdes outlines the strategies women most often use to set the seduction in motion.[40] Lowndes calls these moves "attention-getting devices," and cites research demonstrating their effectiveness. Top moves include: "Smile at him broadly; keep a fixed gaze on him; look at him, toss your head, then look back; and 'accidentally' brush up against him." You'll note that these are all relatively subtle maneuvers. Still, women are often too shy to attempt even these. Don't be. As Lowdes points out, even if you do employ one of these attention-getting devices, chances are good that the man won't remember you did. He'll remember that he boldly came over to talk to you, not that you were brave enough to smile at him and extend an implicit invitation.

Some people are so guarded, they're not even willing to respond when someone else makes the first move. If, miracle of miracles, someone actually comes over to flirt with them despite their stony silence, their admirer is quickly discouraged because they aren't shown any interest. Flirting is a team sport; you can't do it alone. If someone passes you the ball, you have to pass it back to keep the game going. One of the many reasons confidence is so critical to finding love is that you have to be able to recognize flirting for what it is. Let's illustrate this with a simple scenario: an attractive man offers to walk a woman to her car. In this instance, a confident woman would immediately know she was being flirted with. She would smile, say thank you, and use the opportunity to flirt right back. A woman lacking in confidence wouldn't believe the cute guy could possibly be flirting with her. She would retreat in fear, terrified that if she did accept his offer, he might know that she likes him. Let me be clear: you want him to know you like him. If you are not willing to respond to romantic signals, don't be surprised when they stop coming.

You can't make finding love someone else's job. You have to go out and find it for yourself. I hate the expression, "You'll find love when you stop looking for it." This is nonsense. It can be true for some people, but the reason for it has nothing to do with a lack of looking. It's the way you look. I highly recommend reviewing the section in Happiness about being happy without a mate. If you are desperately seeking someone to love, yes, it will make love harder to find. If you are looking for love because you won't be happy without it, it will be harder to find. If you are looking for love because you have low self-esteem and you think it'll make you feel better about yourself, it will be harder to find. You have to look for love the same way you would look for a great new outfit. Have fun trying on a bunch of different looks, and be happy whether or not you find one to take home with you. An expression I do like is, "Date for fun, not to find the one." You can't treat every first date like an interview for marriage and expect to get very far. Just relax and have a good time, no matter who you're with.

There are countless ways to look for love. Go to all the parties you're invited to. Do activities that expose you to a lot of people. Sign up for an online dating service. Online dating has lost a lot of the stigma it once had and there are estimates that 30% of couples now meet that way. Do you think going after love takes away some of the magic? I assure you that it doesn't. Love is magical, and once you're in it you won't care how you got there. I don't love Adam any less because I was the one who pursued him. I just count my lucky stars that I was brave enough to do it.

What Is the Reality of the Situation?

"Man is a reasoning, rather than a reasonable, animal." –
Alexander Hamilton

I am forever amazed by the power of denial. For example: "Yes, I see that this person I'm dating is completely wrong for me and doesn't treat me well, but I'm going to continue dating him anyway." Or: "Yes, I hate being a lawyer and I hate working such long hours, but I'm going to keep doing it anyway." These two hypothetical people, and everyone like them, tell themselves the same lie over and over again: "It's not that bad."

We human beings are not rational creatures. We can usually see the objective facts of a situation: things aren't going well, we're not happy, et cetera. But when our emotions become involved, we come up with all kinds of clever ways to rationalize the facts away. And really, when aren't our emotions involved? In one fascinating study of college students in romantic relationships, the students were able to accurately assess the issues they had in their relationship but misjudged the longevity of the relationship, thinking it would last longer than it did.[41] Friends and parents made more accurate predictions—they saw the same problems the couple did but were able to view the situation without emotion. Your friends and family can tell you that your boyfriend is a jerk or your girlfriend treats you badly because your friends and family aren't in love. Love is a wonderful thing when it's right, but when it's wrong it has an uncanny way of disabling our ability to see reason.

In the case of the overworked lawyer, or anyone in a similarly miserable professional situation, they might not be emotionally attached to their job, but they might be emotionally attached to having a powerful career and a huge salary. Or they could be emotionally attached to all the time and money spent on law school. Leaving behind a career they've spent years (miserable years) working to establish would be hard. Leaving behind a career they've spent a small fortune in graduate school to become qualified for would be hard. Much easier to pretend to love the law.

We spend a lot of time wishing things were different. Wishing our boyfriend was nicer to us, or wishing our boss wasn't so crazy. Or we think back to how things used to be and wish they could be the same. Rather than focus on the present situation, we live in the rose-colored past or the imagined bright future. I could leave, but things used to be so good. I could leave, but things might get better. Difficult though it may be, you have to see things for what they are today. Is it reasonable to think the situation might get better? Is there any evidence that improvement is a legitimate possibility? If there is, work towards improving it. If not, start working on an escape plan.

In many cases, it's just easier to pretend a bad situation doesn't exist then to work on finding a solution. A person with diabetes and high blood pressure knows they should be eating right and exercising, but it doesn't feel good to pass up the cheeseburgers and cupcakes. It's much easier to pretend they're perfectly healthy. A person with massive amounts of debt really shouldn't be shopping, but it wouldn't feel good to not buy that perfect dress, so they tell themselves they'll start saving next month. As Ayn Rand once said, "You can avoid reality, but you cannot avoid the consequences of reality." The longer you deny the existence of a problem, the worse the problem will become. A manageable problem can become a catastrophe if left unchecked. Don't wait until you have a heart attack or have to file for bankruptcy to make some changes.

Are there any facts you've been trying to ignore in your own life? If you're not happy, if something's not working, admit it to yourself and start moving towards a solution. If it's a problem you can fix, then fix it. If it's a situation that you can't, then leave it. There is always something you can do to move yourself closer to where you want to be, but only if you're honest about where you want to go.

Make Success an Option

Occasionally I come across people who have set their lives up in such a way that it's impossible for them to be happy. They accepted a job with an absurdly long commute, or they moved to a small town when they'd much prefer the city. Sometimes in life we wind up in difficult situations, but if you know at the outset that something is going to make you miserable, make a different choice.

Often people will accept a situation they know will make themselves unhappy for the sake of a spouse or a child. It's an admirable and altruistic intention, but one that is sure to backfire. Even the most selfless among us will eventually feel the strain of an untenable situation. Your spouse will not be happy if you are miserable. Your children will not be happy if you are miserable. They might be in the short run, but long term, having a happy partner or parent is infinitely more important. You can't be a good to those you love if you're not taking care of yourself first.

Relationship Responsibility
"We teach people how to treat us." – Dr. Phil McGraw

People generally find it most difficult to accept responsibility when it comes to their personal relationships. After all, you can't control how other people behave. Or can you? You can't force people to behave as you'd like them to, that much is true. But you can control your own behavior, and you will be amazed by how much a change in your own behavior can change a relationship.

I love the idea that "we teach people how to treat us." I first came across this concept when I was young and single and dating all these guys who treated me terribly. I thought somehow I was attracting all the jerks in the world, never thinking that I might have had something to do with it. When someone treated me badly I just accepted it, and in doing so I was showing them that their behavior was okay with me. I was teaching them that they could behave however they wanted and I wouldn't stop them. Once I decided to be a doormat, is it any wonder they treated me as one? If you don't hold someone accountable for their behavior, why should they hold themselves accountable?

One of the best books I've read on the subject is Amy Sutherland's *What Shamu Taught Me About Life, Love, and Marriage*.[42] It's a witty book that describes how useful animal training techniques can be in managing human relationships. Everyone knows that if you want your dog to heel or roll over and play dead, you're going to have to teach him, and if you don't want the dog to pee on your carpet, you're going to have to stop him. But few of us recognize the role we play in "training" the people in our lives how to behave. As Sutherland puts it:

> "Any interaction is training. Every time you have any kind of contact with an animal you are teaching it something whether you mean to or not."

Even though she's talking about animals here, the point still holds. Whenever we interact with someone, we are giving them feedback. We're teaching them what we like, what we don't like, and what we're willing to put up with.

As the expression goes, "Fool me once, shame on you, fool me twice, shame on me." If someone treats you badly and you continue to let them behave that way, at some point it becomes your own fault. Bad behavior should have consequences. You can't make it another person's responsibility to know that you are upset, and you can't expect someone to change until you ask them to.

Further, whether or not we agree with it, people always have a reason for behaving the way they do. What are they getting out of it? And, more importantly, how might you be contributing to it? One of my friends had a boyfriend who refused to prepare for anything until the eleventh hour, forcing her to rush in and save the day. That behavior only stopped when she stopped saving the day. If someone's bad behavior results in them getting what they want, why would they change?

People will also follow your example. You have to behave the way you want someone else to behave. You have to be kind and loving and understanding if you expect the same from someone else. A lot of times couples get caught in a stalemate. They think, "Why should I do something nice for my spouse when she never does anything nice for me?" You have to give before you can receive. Devote yourself to your partner. Make their happiness your first priority. Chances are, they will respond in kind. If you are truly treating your spouse like a king or queen and they don't reciprocate, then you have a problem. But start with your own behavior first.

Further, sometimes we unintentionally punish people for doing the very things we want them to do. I had a relative who would criticize me every time I called. She would tell me what terrible mistakes she thought I was making in my life, and how I'd be so much happier if only I listened to her advice. And then she would berate me for not calling her more often. If she really wanted me to call more often, an effective strategy would have been to make the times I did call more enjoyable experiences. If you want someone to repeat a behavior, give them a reason they should.

There will be times when you won't be able to change someone's behavior. As Sutherland puts it, "Trainers know that some behaviors are so hardwired, they may never be trained away." At that point, you are going to have to decide if you can live with the behavior or not. It might help you respond more calmly to the wet towel on the floor if you know you're not going to leave your marriage over it. If someone's behavior is truly unacceptable, leaving may be your only option.

It's very tempting to blame our problems with other people on other people, but responsibility equals power. When you take responsibility for another person's behavior, you give yourself the power to change it.

Save Yourself

"It is better to light a candle than to curse the darkness." – Chinese Proverb

On occasion, we all get some really bad luck. There will be times when things go wrong through no fault of your own. You could be walking around minding your own business when you fall into a giant hole you never could have seen coming. The question then becomes, how will you respond? You can sit there and complain. You can curse the universe for putting the hole in your way. You can look at your cuts and bruises and say you're too hurt to move. You can cross your fingers and hope someone comes by with a ladder. Or you can start clawing your way out. It might not be your fault you fell in that hole, but it is still your responsibility to get yourself out. Yes, it might suck that you're going to have to put all this effort and energy into fixing a problem you didn't create. It might feel deeply unfair.

Why did this have to happen to you? What did you do to deserve this? The unfortunate thing is that it doesn't matter. Bad things happen sometimes. In life, the most important lessons we learn are often painful ones. One day you might discover there was a great reason why you had to go through all that trouble. But you're not going to know what it is right away. For now, all you can do is focus on finding a way out.

It's easy to start feeling sorry for yourself when things don't go your way, and it's easy to use a setback as a reason to give up. When someone isn't successful – and isn't doing anything about it – they usually have a situation or an incident they point to as an excuse for their failure: "Well, I would have been a professional athlete, but I had an injury during my draft year" or "I want to become a doctor, but I'm too old to go to medical school." You will always be able to find someone who was in your situation and succeeded anyway. Why did they succeed? Because they were able to look past their circumstances and take responsibility for their success, even when they had a great excuse to blame their failure on something else. No one has ever made a movie about someone who gave up when things got hard.

Let Go of the Past

"When one door closes another opens. But we often look so long and so regretfully upon the closed door that we fail to see the one that has opened for us." – Alexander Graham Bell

Who you are right now doesn't have to have anything to do with who you used to be, where you came from, or what has happened to you in the past. No matter what has happened in your life, your past cannot define your future unless you let it.

Many people have had terrible childhoods. Some use their past as motivation to pursue a better future. Others use the past as a reason to stay in a terrible place. A good friend of mine was a foster child, and had a very difficult time of it, as is unfortunately the case for many foster children. She had a mother that didn't want her and a foster family that didn't care for her. There was also a boy living with her foster family in much the same circumstance. My friend put herself through college and graduate school and went on to have a successful career, a caring husband, and two lovely children. Her foster brother had a lifetime of drug problems and is currently incarcerated. I know my friend struggles with guilt over the situation. How was she able to defy her past when her foster brother was not? I know there are probably many factors, but one of them was certainly my friend's willingness to take responsibility for her life. She didn't expect anyone to help her. For her, the neglect fostered a strong self-reliance. I'm not suggesting that it was easy. I know that it wasn't. But given the choice between giving up and struggling on, she struggled on, and she now continues to reap the benefits of that struggle.

To become the best version of who you are now, you have to let go of any negative feelings you have about what has happened in the past. It can be a difficult thing to do. It may feel as though you are letting anyone who has wronged you "win" by letting go of the grudge. But when you blame someone else for where you are today, you are keeping them a part of your life. You are giving them power. As I've said before, power and responsibility go hand-in-hand. If you want the power to change your life, you have to take responsibility for it. You may not be responsible for what happened to you, but you are responsible for how you cope with it.

As I noted in the chapter on Focus, we move in the direction we're looking. If you're looking back, you can't move forward. You have to leave the past behind before you can get to where you want to be.

Caveat

Know When Not to Take Responsibility
"I don't deserve this award, but I have arthritis and I don't deserve that either." - Jack Benny

Taking responsibility for your life does not mean blaming yourself for things that were not your fault. A friend of mine recently escaped an abusive relationship. I remember her worrying over her role in the situation. I'll say now what I said to her then: there is nothing she could have said or done that would have justified violence. She could have been the worst girlfriend in the world, and it would not have entitled him to strike her. I always applaud a willingness to see your own part in a bad situation, but there are circumstances in which you will do yourself more harm than good if you blame yourself. You can take responsibility for getting out of a bad situation or picking yourself back up when you fall down, but please don't blame yourself for every bad thing that happens. Sometimes it's just not your fault.

Failure or Bad Luck?

There are good plans that will fail due to bad luck. It doesn't mean that they weren't good plans. As I mentioned in the introduction to this section, some people feel that if they work hard enough or plan well enough, luck won't play any part in their life. It's just not true. Much as you might want to, you can't control everything. Luck will be a factor in everything you do. When something goes wrong, honestly assess the role that luck had to play. Your actions may have had nothing to do with it. Of course, the same can be said for good luck – even a bad plan can succeed if your luck is good enough. It doesn't mean you should try things the same way again next time. Luck always plays a role, and sometimes a decisive one. Getting down on yourself for something you couldn't control is a waste of time and energy and it will make it harder for you to move on. Sometimes it is just bad luck.

TENET #9: AWARENESS

"Let us not look back in anger, nor forward in fear, but around us in awareness." – *James Thurber*

If you want to be lucky, you must first become a student of your own life. Clues for how to make yourself a luckier person are all around you. You get feedback all the time from the people in your life, from the outcomes of your actions, and even from your own unconscious mind. In many different forms, you get information about what is working and what isn't. If you can look to your past and see what has brought you either success or failure, you can learn which behaviors you should keep and which to eliminate. If you can use the feedback from the people you interact with to better tailor your communication, your relationships can improve. If you can learn to listen to the little voice in your head, you can make better decisions. You likely already have all the information you need to make the most of your life. The world around you is a roadmap to your success.

Awareness of Yourself

"Until we see what we are, we cannot take steps to become what we should be." – Charlotte Perkins Gilman

I love the book *Committed*, by Elizabeth Gilbert.[43] I enjoy it so much because it is Gilbert's attempt to get comfortable with the idea of marriage before entering into her second one. I relate to her struggle for obvious reasons – as a divorcee I was terrified of getting married again. I didn't think I would get divorced the first time around, so why should the second time be any different? Also, aren't there all those statistics about how those who have been divorced once are much more likely to get divorced again? It turns out that one divorce doesn't necessarily lead to more – it's only those who aren't able to fix their own problems that are destined for repeated trips down the aisle. As Gilbert puts it:

> "The problem comes when people carry unresolved destructive behaviors with them from one marriage to the next – such as alcoholism, compulsive gambling, mental illness, violence, or philandering. With baggage like that, it really doesn't matter whom you marry, because you're going to wreck that relationship eventually and inevitably, based on your own pathologies."

I found that information enormously encouraging. None of those factors led to the end of my first marriage. I can hardly claim to have been a great wife to my ex-husband at all times, but divorce has a way of teaching you some valuable lessons. After reading *Committed*, I felt I had a better chance at sustaining a marriage than I did the first time around.

The point I'm trying to convey with this story is that we are all destined to repeat any mistakes we aren't able to correct. If someone goes from one relationship to the next without stopping to see how their own issues might be contributing to the problems they're having with partners, they have no reason to believe that their "luck" will improve in the future. This is particularly the case if the relationship always ends for the same reason. The relationship starts out great, but then the same problems rear their ugly heads. One of the major issues I had with my ex-husband was that he didn't consistently make me his first priority. I truly hope he doesn't make the same mistake with his next wife, but if he does I wouldn't be surprised if that marriage ends in divorce as well. If your current significant other starts complaining about the same things your last significant other did, take notice.

Similarly, if you find you encounter the same difficulties in any area of your life over and over again, you have to explore the possibility that your behavior could be the problem. Some of the least lucky people I know are those that cannot see how their behavior is contributing to the situation. They bring the same issues into every encounter and are dismayed when it doesn't go their way. They feel profoundly unlucky when, really, it has nothing to do with luck. It can be uncomfortable to admit that you might be the problem, but if you are the problem, you can also be the solution. As I suggested in the previous chapter, when you take responsibility for a situation, you give yourself the power to change it. If you can change, you can stop waiting for your luck to change.

Therapy can be enormously useful if you continually find yourself experiencing the same "bad luck." Friends and family will often be too polite to tell you about your destructive behaviors. If you don't know you have a problem, they won't see it as their place to tell you that you do. A therapist can provide you with an honest and impartial point of view. It's their job to help you see how you might be creating your own bad luck.

Awareness of Your Impact on Others

"I tried telling him without telling him, through body language, and I observed he was unobservant." – Jarod Kintz, A Zebra is the Piano of the Animal Kingdom

In the previous section, I spoke about how destructive behavior can impact your life in a global way. If someone is narcissistic, for example, that is likely have a long-standing negative effect on many aspects of their life. What I want to discuss in this section is something much more subtle: how people respond to you in your everyday interactions. The conversation you have with our coworker while making coffee. The small talk you make with a neighbor at the supermarket. Your first encounter with someone you find attractive at a party.

A lot of your success with other people begins and ends with your ability to read how what you say and do affects them. Being able to read the facial expressions and body language of those around you is the ticket to enduring success both socially and professionally. If you cannot tell if you're pleasing someone, or boring someone, or offending someone, you're bound to encounter problems. Let's imagine a situation where a man inadvertently says something that offends the woman he's speaking with. Let's say he guesses the woman he's talking to is 35 years of age, when she's really only 30. A person who is aware of the affect his words have had will find a way to smooth the situation over, saying something like, "You've accomplished so much in your career that I didn't think you could possibly be younger. I'm so impressed!" There are those, whoever, who might be too absorbed in their own thoughts to notice the miffed expression on the woman's face. They'll keep talking about themselves, not noticing that they've made a mistake, and when the conversation is over the woman will walk away feeling insulted and she won't have a very high opinion of the man who insulted her.

So many people are focused inwardly when interacting with others. They're thinking about what they're going to say next, they're focused on their own feelings, or their mind wanders to something totally unrelated to the conversation. They aren't listening closely to what the other person has to say, and worse, they are not monitoring the non-verbal signals the other person is sending. Most people aren't going to tell you if you've offended them, or if you're talking too much, or if they're not interested in what you're saying. They're not going to say "I find you socially awkward" or "What you're saying is really strange." But they will provide you with all of that feedback and more with their body language and the expression on their face.

Here are some quick tips on developing better awareness:

(1) **Watch the Face**. People are unable to consciously control their facial expressions. Even if they try, there will always be an instant when they first react to

something when their true feelings are plainly apparent on their face. If you stay attuned to facial expressions, you can gain valuable insight into how someone is responding to you. The expressions that connote happiness, sadness, anger, surprise, fear and disgust are universal. You could stumble upon a previously undiscovered tribe in the Amazon rainforest and be able to tell how they're feeling. If someone looks happy, keep saying what you're saying, but if someone looks angry or upset, backpedal ASAP.

(2) **Watch the Eyes**. If someone is maintaining eye contact with you that's a good sign. But if someone is looking everywhere but at you, that's a very bad sign. Chances are that if they're scanning the room they're looking for someone they'd rather be talking to. Find a topic of conversation your partner would find more interesting. Hint: most people's favorite topic is themselves.

(3) **Watch the Eyebrows**. Raised eyebrows indicate surprise or disbelief, while lowered eyebrows indicate puzzlement or anger. If someone's eyebrows are super high or low, you might want to steer the conversation another way.

(4) **Watch the Smile**. There is a simple way to tell whether someone's smile is genuine or not: does their smile reach their eyes? If you put your hand over the bottom half of their face, could you still tell that they are smiling? Genuine happiness or amusement comes through in the eyes.

(5) **Watch the Body**. Even when they're not talking, people are always saying something with their body language. Fidgeting is a sign of boredom. When someone is uncomfortable, they'll raise their shoulders. Someone

crossing their arms in front of their chest is a classic sign that they're closed off – perhaps from you, perhaps from people in general. Positive signs? If someone is enjoying your company they will have a relaxed and open stance and face you directly rather than at an angle.

(6) **Watch the Space**. The amount of space between you and the person you're speaking with is another important signal. Generally speaking, the less space the better. If someone is interested in you – particularly if the interest is romantic – they'll move in closer to you, lean into you, possibly even so close that you're touching. Close proximity is only a bad sign if they are trying to bully or intimidate you. Someone who doesn't want to be talking to you will slowly start to edge away.

When you learn to respond to the positive and negative signals someone sends you, you stand a much better chance at having the person you're talking to enjoy the conversation, thus increasing your odds of turning that conversation into an ongoing relationship.

Monitoring non-verbal signals is most critical in the early stages of a relationship, but it's a good idea to stay attuned to them even if you've known someone for a long time. Friends, family, and lovers won't always tell you if you've upset them or if you're behaving in a way they don't like. The more time you spend with someone, the better the opportunity you have to learn their patterns. What do they do when they get upset? Is their tone of voice colder? Do they stop smiling? Will they avoid eye contact? Will they snap at you over something unrelated? You may think it's the responsibility of the other person to tell you what is bothering them. It is important to foster honest and open communication. But that doesn't absolve you of a responsibility to pay attention. A person may not feel comfortable telling you directly that he or she is upset. They might be afraid that you'll get angry, or they might feel silly bringing it up. If problems are ignored, they can grow and quickly spiral out of control. Even small problems can become big ones if left to fester. If you want to have happy, successful, lasting relationships, you must learn to read the signs.

Awareness of People

"Manners are a sensitive awareness of the feelings of others. If you have that awareness, you have good manners, no matter what fork you use." – Emily Post

Being aware of other people goes beyond noticing how they respond to you. The same skills you develop to monitor someone's responses to what you say can be used to better understand how they feel about other people and situations. What someone tells you with their eyes, their expressions, and their body language is much more important than what they say with their words.

In her book, *How to Be a People Magnet*[44], Leil Lowndes describes a fascinating study of children that demonstrated that a child's ability to read and respond to others' body language and tones of voice was directly related to how popular they were.[45] It's easy to see how that might be the case, and I'm certain the same could be said of adults. People like nothing more than to be understood without having to explicitly tell you what they're feeling. Most people won't come out and say something like, "I'm upset about this," especially if they don't know you very well. But if you can understand and respond to their mood before you respond to their words, you will find that people are grateful for it. It's much easier to hide what you are feeling with your words than with your expressions, so when someone's words don't match their expressions, trust the expressions. If someone is clearly upset, gently ask them about it.

Awareness of Audience

When you're interacting with other people, one strategy will not fit all. Just as every product on the shelves and every show on TV are designed to appeal to a particular audience, everything you say should be tailored to the person you're speaking with. What makes one person happy might annoy another, and vice versa.

In a job I had years ago, I had two female supervisors, both of whom reported to the same man, the head of our department. Let's call him Ken. Both of these women were excellent at what they did, but they nonetheless had very different relationships with Ken. One woman, let's call her Anne, had a positive relationship with Ken. They worked well together with little strife. The other woman, let's call her Brenda, had a terrible relationship with Ken. They were constantly arguing. Ken was a talented man in many ways, but, unfortunately, he was in possession of a rather fragile ego. If you made him feel threatened in any way, by suggesting he might be wrong about something, for example, he reacted by lashing out. If, however, you made him feel smart and important, he would love you. The trick was to know how to deal with him and act accordingly. Anne knew that while it might at times seem ridiculous and burdensome to have to be so gentle with Ken's ego, it was well worth the effort in the long run. Brenda, however, felt that placating Ken was beneath her – and she paid the price for it, over and over again.

In a perfect world, none of us would ever have to bolster our boss's self-esteem in order to have a pleasant working relationship, but this is not a perfect world. In the real world, it pays to know who you're dealing with. If you want to have a positive relationship with your supervisors, or in-laws, or clients, you have to know what makes them happy. Be aware of what they respond to positively, and what makes them angry or sad. Remember that information for the next time so you can better tailor your interactions to suit them.

Awareness of Norms

Whether we recognize it or not, much of our lives are determined by norms. There are unwritten rules governing just about every situation. We all know to say "hello" when we answer the phone and "thank you" when someone does us a favor. We know we should bring something when we're invited to someone's house for a party. We know that we shouldn't cut in line. We know to turn off our cell phones in movie theaters. And we're all aware of the uproar that ensues if someone doesn't comply. We don't think of these as rules, but we are constantly guided by our own sense of social decorum. The question becomes, what happens when we walk into a situation where we don't know the rules?

The best strategy when entering any new environment is to sit back and absorb your surroundings. People aren't going to tell you what the norms of a group are, but I assure you that there will be some. Each group and each team and each organization has its own culture: which topics are taboo, how much you are allowed to drink, if swearing is okay, whether it's acceptable to talk about politics. If you break one of the rules before you know what they are, you are sending the group a strong signal that says, "I am not one of you." First impressions are powerful. You want someone's first impression of you to be "S/he fits in here. S/he's just like me."

I don't want it to sound like I'm advocating conformity as a general rule. I absolutely think it's important to be yourself and be confident in who you are. But it's also important to find a way to fit in before you find a way to stand out. In some areas of our life we have the freedom to find people who are compatible with us and the freedom to ignore or avoid those that aren't. But in many, many other areas we don't have that luxury. There will always be people we have to get along with, like it or not. When you play on a team you have to get along with your teammates. When you start dating someone new you have to get along with their friends and family. In any workplace, you have to get along with your co-workers, and if you have your own business, you have to get along with your clients. It's always a good idea to watch and learn when you're the new guy. When you go out for drinks with your coworkers for the first time, see how they interact before you jump into the conversation. Use the opportunity to learn what a typical night is for them. I rarely went out with my old coworkers, and when we did, we'd have a drink or two then head out the door. I have a friend, however, that gets drunk with her colleagues every Thursday night as a matter of course. Different environments have different rules. You have to learn what they are if you want to play along.

Awareness of Intuition

"I feel there are two people inside of me – me and my intuition. If I go against her, she'll screw me every time, and if I follow her, we get along quite nicely." – Kim Basinger

I'm sure you've had the experience of knowing in your gut that what you were doing was right or what you were doing was wrong. You've probably also ignored that feeling at one time or another and wound up paying the price for it. It can be easy to doubt your intuition. It is just a feeling, after all. It isn't a fact or a well-reasoned argument. As a society we don't have a lot of respect for decisions based on feelings alone. People believe that if you don't know how you came to a particular conclusion, the conclusion can't be valid. But as it turns out, your feelings might be based on a lot more facts than you realize.

Malcolm Gladwell's book, *Blink*, is a wonderful and thorough exploration of what goes into making snap decisions – decisions you arrive at immediately, for which you can't logically explain.[46] Gladwell argues that in many cases making decisions based on a gut feeling is just as good – and often better – than decisions based on facts alone. The reason for this is that our brains are a lot more powerful than we give them credit for. They are information absorbing machines. We are very selective about our conscious thoughts and observations. We can only pay attention to one thing at a time and must let everything else fade into the background. But our unconscious minds can process many things at once. Not only do our unconscious minds notice and record more information than we realize, but they are able to use that information to draw conclusions without us knowing how. We might be able to reason our way to the same conclusion eventually, but we'd take a lot longer and require a lot more information.

Gladwell describes an experiment conducted by the University of Iowa in which participants were asked to pick cards from two red decks and two blue decks.[47] Each card represented either a monetary gain or a loss, and the goal of the exercise was to make as much money as possible. Picking blue cards was the way to go – the losses on the cards in the blue decks were less than the gains. The question was how long it would take the participants to figure it out. After drawing about fifty cards, participants started to get a feeling the red cards were the problem, and by about eighty cards they understood the game. Fascinatingly, participants started showing a stress response when picking from the red piles in as few as ten cards. Our brains aren't just a bit quicker than we are, but much, much quicker than we are. What interests me most about the experiment, however, is not what happens at ten cards, but what happens between cards fifty and eighty: the time between when a hunch is developed and a conclusion is reached. What if they had stopped the experiment after the participants drew fifty cards? They already had a hunch that the blue cards were the way to go, but they wouldn't have been able to tell you why exactly. Their *conclusion*, however, would have been just as valid at fifty cards as it was at eighty. Many times in your own life, you're only going to get fifty cards. You're going have to make decisions based on incomplete information. And yet, as this experiment illustrates, your gut feelings could be leading you to the same decisions you'd make if you had all the time and information in the world.

It's as though your brain is constantly gathering puzzle pieces that you might never need and likely will never know are there. When you're faced with a decision, your brain is able to rummage through millions of those hidden little pieces and put together a picture. When I worked as a statistical analyst, I used my computer to serve the same function. I would feed it thousands and thousands of data points and then ask it a question. The computer would spit back a conclusion in a matter of moments that would've taken me months to reach by hand. But unlike my computer, your brain isn't able to give you numbers and a clear answer. All it can give you is a feeling. It's like a Magic 8 Ball: it will only say "Yes," "No," or, "Ask again later." It's very easy to ignore that kind of fuzzy advice. Or worse, get so caught up in your conscious thoughts that you don't even bother to ask yourself how you're feeling. In many cases, our feelings are the best information we have. They're based on a lot more data than our thoughts.

When you need to make a decision or evaluate a situation, the facts are important. Of course they are. You should review whatever data you have and do your best to come to a "logical" conclusion. I would just suggest that while you're doing your research, you periodically stop to ask yourself how you're feeling. Your mind is trying to tell you things all the time. It has way more information than you do, but it can't speak with you directly, and it can't force you to heed its message. You can go ahead and disregard its wisdom, but I wouldn't advise it. Trust your instincts.

Caveat

Awareness versus Mind-Reading

It's important to make the distinction between being aware of someone's emotions and guessing why they are feeling those emotions. Some people make the mistake of seeing someone who is upset and automatically assuming that they are the ones who upset them. When you see that someone is upset, ask them what's going on. Gently. And then listen to their answer. You can see and be aware of the emotion. You cannot know why they are feeling that emotion without more information.

You Don't Always Have to Conform

There's nothing wrong with going your own way and standing out from the crowd. You don't always have to behave according the norms of the group. It's just worth considering what your rebellion may cost you before you do. Make your defiance a choice rather than an accident.

Problem Instincts

Instincts based on your brain power take some time to develop. The idea is that your brain gathers information over time and then comes to a conclusion. When you have an automatic reaction to an unfamiliar situation or a person you just met, it is not likely to be based on much data. I wouldn't go so far as to suggest that you ignore your gut reactions. It's not always possible to explain how we "know" things. I just wouldn't be quite as quick to trust them.

BETH BRUDER

TENET #10: SERENITY

"Life is a series of natural and spontaneous changes. Don't resist them; that only creates sorrow. Let reality be reality. Let things flow naturally forward in whatever way they like." – Lao Tzu

Most of this book is about doing what you can to get the best possible luck; this chapter is about getting out of your own way. Just as there are ways that you can tip the odds in your favor, there are ways for you to stack the odds against yourself. The two habits most likely to undermine your best efforts are anxiety and anger. Anxiety is an anathema to your quality of life, and can even make what you want harder to get. Anger is a destructive force that can scare away any good luck that might have been coming your way. Learn how to control your nerves and your temper and you will be well on your way to living the life of your dreams.

Don't Worry

"Fear is pain arising from the anticipation of evil." – Aristotle

People waste so much time and energy worrying. They worry about what might happen. They worry about what might not happen. They worry that they will fail. They worry about what will happen if they succeed. If things are good, they worry that they will suddenly go wrong, and if things are bad, they worry that they will never improve. The question is, why does anyone worry at all when it's so obvious that the worry itself won't help anything?

Personally, I think people worry because they want to be prepared. When something goes wrong, they find comfort in thinking, "Well, I knew this was going to happen." They feel that if they get their hopes up and allow themselves to believe that everything is just fine, that it will hurt all the more if things go wrong. If something bad does happen, it might hurt. You might suffer. But that's not a good enough reason to suffer over something that hasn't happened yet and might never happen. Preparation involves practical things like making sure you packed the sunblock and your passport. It doesn't involve practicing how much it's going to hurt if something were to go wrong.

There are also those who feel that if they aren't always on their guard, they might miss something and then fail because they weren't paying attention. They maintain constant, anxiety-laden vigilance even when none is required. Meanwhile, all that anxiety keeps them from appreciating the life they are so afraid to lose. It's nearly impossible to enjoy yourself if you are worried all the time. What use would good luck be to you if it didn't make you any happier? What would it matter if something went wrong if you aren't having any fun anyway? When you are anxious, you are choosing to diminish your own quality of life. You can immediately be happier – *and feel luckier* – today if you can stop worrying about tomorrow.

Rather than living in fear of what *might* happen, foster the belief that whatever *does* happen, you will always be alright. No matter what, life will go on and you will be fine. Think back to the most difficult times in your life. More likely than not you can point to some reason why it was important that the bad things happened, or at the very least, that there was something to be gained from the experience. We are all a product of our experiences, and none of us would be who we are if we hadn't had to learn difficult lessons. Meaning can be found in even the most tragic of events.

Throughout the time when I was getting divorced, I kept a journal. More accurately, I kept several journals, eventually filling four notebooks. By the time I started the fourth notebook, I was a profoundly different person than when I had started the first. I had done so much reading and growing and I was finally living my life in a way I could be proud of. Starting that fourth notebook felt significant. It felt like I'd come to the end of the transition, and I was starting the next phase of my life. I remember thinking at the time that I would only record the "good things" that happened in my notebook. I wanted to focus on the positive, and I didn't want to waste any time or energy writing about the bad things that happened. And that's when I realized they were all good things. I could look back to the disappointments I had written about in the previous journals, all of the bumps in the road and things that hadn't gone the way I'd wanted them to, and I could see how things had to happen the way they did. I wrote in Flexibility about the concept of "lucky failure," how we often find ourselves glad we didn't get what we wanted because it opened the door to something better. When I re-read my journals, I saw how all of my disappointments cleared the way for better opportunities. The bad things turned into good things.

We're not always going to get what we want, and it's rarely immediately apparent why something bad happens when it does. If you can develop the attitude that even the bad things will be good ones eventually, it becomes a lot easier not to worry about what might be. Belief is important to luck, and anxiety is a lack of belief.

Serenity for Beauty and Health

"The mere apprehension of a coming evil has put many into a situation of the utmost danger." – Lucan

Two obvious components of good luck are good health and good looks. We don't often see sick and unattractive people and wish we had their luck. When working towards creating a luckier life for yourself, these areas aren't a bad place to start, and these two birds can be killed with one stone if you're able to become more serene. I'm sure you've heard it many times before, but I would be remiss if I didn't reiterate the following: stress is bad for your health and bad for your appearance.

Evolutionarily, your body's stress response was designed to help you out when you faced immediate danger.

The danger your body is prepared to face is a short-term threat that can be resolved with a physical reaction, such as running or fighting (i.e. the famed "fight or flight" response). When you're under stress, your body responds as though you're being chased by a bear. Your senses are heightened, your heart rate, respiration and blood pressure all go up, and your bloodstream is flooded with sugar to give you extra energy. Further, your body shuts down all the systems you won't need when you're in immediate danger, including your immune, digestive, and reproductive systems. If you were actually running from a bear, this would all be very helpful. But I'm guessing you don't encounter many bears.

Rather, your stressors these days are more likely constant than intermittent. Common examples are a stressful job, financial problems, relationship problems, or caring for an aging parent. Your stress response system wasn't meant to be activated that often. If these responses were few and far between, it wouldn't matter that your blood pressure is raised and your non-essential systems are shut down. But on a day-to-day basis, it matters that your blood pressure is high. It matters that your immune system is impaired. It matters that your digestion is disrupted. It matters that your sex drive and reproductive capabilities are impeded. Frequent stress has been linked with the following health problems:

- Heart Disease
- Stroke
- Type 2 Diabetes
- Greater Susceptibility to Illness
- Slower Wound Healing
- Gastrointestinal Disorders
- Rheumatoid Arthritis

- Decreased Bone Density
- Decreased Muscle Tissue
- Infertility
- Depression
- Insomnia
- Substance Abuse

The effects of stress can also wreak havoc on your physical appearance. First and foremost, increased levels of cortisol, the primary stress hormone, have been linked to increased appetite, sugar cravings, and weight gain in animals and humans. Not only does it contribute to weight gain, but it leads to the accumulation of visceral fat, the kind of fat that surrounds the organs in the abdominal cavity (e.g. stomach, liver, kidneys). Visceral fat has been shown to be much more harmful to your health than the kind found elsewhere on the body and is strongly associated with insulin resistance and Type-2 Diabetes. Not to mention the fact that pot bellies are not attractive. And then there is the effect stress has on your skin. Too much cortisol leads to damage to our skin's collagen, which in turn leads to wrinkles and premature aging. Further, stress has been shown to trigger or worsen conditions such as acne, psoriasis, rosacea, and fever blisters. Dermatologists have found that treating both the stress and the skin condition together leads to better results than treating the skin alone.

I wanted this all to sound as scary as possible so that it becomes painfully clear how important it is to reduce the amount of stress in your life. So many of us push ourselves to pack more and more into every day and don't place enough importance on rest and relaxation. I know that most people are pressed for time these days, but how many of the things that take up our time are truly critical? Is running an extra errand or fitting in one more sales call really worth hurting your health and appearance? When you're thinking about adding another class or social obligation to your calendar, ask yourself if it's really worth becoming sick and less attractive. I want you to know how critical it is to make your mental health and well-being a priority. Don't wait until you get sick to make a change. Don't wait until you're prematurely old and gray to make a change. Take it seriously right now.

Stress Relief

"He that fears not the future may enjoy the present." – Thomas Fuller

Below you'll find a few suggestions for getting some of the stress out of our life. There are, of course, numerous resources on the Internet and elsewhere out there if you'd like some additional strategies.

(1) **Physical Activity**. Exercise is an excellent way to directly reduce levels of cortisol and all those other nasty stress hormones. As I mentioned in the previous section, your body thinks that you're going to respond physically when you face a stressful event. It thinks you're running away from that bear. So if you go out for a run when you're stressed, you're giving your body what it wants, and you're making it a lot easier for your system to return to normal.

(2) **Sleep.** Sleep plays a critical role in the body's regulation of cortisol. Ordinarily, cortisol levels are highest in the

morning and lowest a few hours after you fall asleep at night. But when you're sleep deprived, your body's natural ability to regulate the amount of cortisol in your blood is thrown out of balance, which can result in chronically high levels. Sleepiness also tends to lead to drinking lots of coffee, which raises cortisol levels even higher. In addition to the effects lack of sleep has on your stress hormones, being sleepy also makes it much more difficult for you to function at your best. It will take you longer to accomplish the same tasks and will lead you to make more mistakes, both of which will likely make you even more stressed.

(3) **Meditation.** If you haven't already heard the news, meditation is really, really good for you. In addition to reducing stress (and all of the health benefits that go along with reduced stress), regular meditation can improve concentration, memory, and reaction time. It can even make you happier.

(4) **Balance.** As I mentioned in the previous section, you can't do it all and expect not to be stressed out. Prioritize and learn how to say no. Your time is a precious and limited resource; don't give it away to things that don't deserve your attention. In the workplace, I know people are often afraid to say no. It can help to recognize that everyone at your workplace will benefit if your time is managed effectively. If you take on so much that you aren't able to complete anything effectively, it will look much worse than if you'd just said no in the first place.

Calm is Contagious

"How very little can be done under the spirit of fear." – Florence Nightingale

One of the most insidious problems caused by anxiety is the effect it has on those around you. Anxiety is contagious. If you feel uncomfortable, those around you will be able to sense it and become uncomfortable themselves. Fortunately, the opposite is true as well: if your demeanor is calm, the people around you will relax, even if they themselves are anxious. Remaining calm is the best way to diffuse any tense situation and to make those around you feel comfortable.

We tend to think very highly of those who are able to remain composed in difficult situations. Leaders often become leaders in times of crisis. When those around them are panicking, leaders are able to remain strong and steady, and in doing so they reassure others that all will be well. Even on an ordinary day when nothing is going wrong, people enjoy being around those who make them feel at ease. So many people are constantly anxious. Interacting with someone who is calm is soothing to them. You can make them feel warm and safe. Little kids are used to being reassured by their parents all the time, and many of us still crave that kind of comfort as adults. If you can fill that role for someone, they will want to keep you a part of their life. They might not even know why they enjoy spending time with you so much, but it's certain that they will.

It's also particularly important to exude calm when you're hoping to seduce someone. Most people get nervous when they meet someone they like. They clam up, have trouble being themselves, and the idea of doing something like kissing someone or asking for a phone number becomes overwhelming. This is why so many people are only able to flirt effectively after they've had a few drinks. You can skip the alcohol and give people this same affect by exuding coolness and confidence. Your own lack of anxiety provides a strong signal that there is nothing to be anxious about. It can be hypnotic. Give them the impression that kissing you would be the most natural thing in the world. And it will be.

Let the Universe Do Its Work

"Waiting is not mere empty hoping. It has the inner certainty of reaching the goal." – I Ching

The vast majority of this book is about doing the things you can do to make yourself lucky. It's about controlling the things that are under your control. But as you well know, you can't control everything. At some point you are going to have to sit back and wait for some good luck.

In some ways, pursing a goal is like gardening. First you have to decide what you want to plant, and then you have to do the work of planting it. You have to dig the hole, sow the seed, water, fertilize, and weed. But then you're just going to have to wait for it to grow. At some point, once you've done everything you can, all you need is time. So often people want instant gratification. If they go on a diet, they want to lose ten pounds in two days. If they go on a date, they want to know immediately if the relationship has a future. If they start a new venture, they want to succeed right away. But the world doesn't work that way. Waiting is an inevitable part of wanting.

Almost always in life there will be a delay between the time when you set a course of action in motion, and the time you are able to see the results of that action. During that time, it's often impossible to know how things will turn out. There are few things people hate more than not knowing what is going to happen next. To be caught in limbo. To know that a change might be coming and know there is nothing they can do about it. If you let it, that uncertainty can feel excruciating. Given how often you likely find yourself waiting for *something*, you could be suffering on a regular basis. In many ways, your very happiness can be determined by how well you are able to wait.

Further, the inability to wait can make what you want harder to get. As Jessica Lange once said, "When you learn not to want things so badly, life comes to you." I love that quote. The more you want something that you don't yet have, the harder it is to be happy without it, and you have to be happy without it in order to get it. If you cannot be happy without something, you are likely to become desperate, and desperation can only lead to trouble. Desperate people give off a desperate energy they can't hide, and no one wants to befriend, or hire, or invest in, or marry a desperate person. Presumably, this is why the expression "you'll find love when you stop looking for it" is such a popular one. As I hope I've made clear, I don't ascribe to that philosophy. I do think you have to look for love if you want it. But you have to look for love *while being happy in your own life*. Desperate people either repel all potential mates or settle for someone who isn't good enough for them. Looking for love should not involve frantic, desperate searching, nor should it involve stopping the search at the first possible opportunity, regardless of how inadequate that opportunity might be.

Being comfortable with uncertainty is also important

because forcing the issue will often do you more harm than good. Let's use interviewing for a job as an example. If they tell you that you'll hear back from them in a week, and you don't hear from them in over a week, it's perfectly appropriate to call and check in. However, if you're calling to see if they've made a decision the day after your interview, all you're going to do is make them less likely to offer you the job.

There is an element of the unknowable in everything. Thinking back to the gardening analogy, you can plant the seed, and you do everything you can to help it grow, but it's the plant itself that has to do the growing. You can't force it. All you can do is hope that the seed comes to life. You can set the conditions for luck. And then your job is to be patient. *Happy* and patient. Once you've done all you can do, the best way to get what you want is to remain calm and confident that the luck you're looking for is on its way.

Slow to Anger

"How much more grievous are the consequences of anger than the causes of it." – Marcus Aurelius

In addition to anxiety, anger is an emotion very likely to make you an unlucky person. Anger is powerful and can thus have a powerful impact on your life. We say and do things in anger that we would never say and do ordinarily, the results of which can be devastating.

Hurting Your Heart

Earlier in this chapter, I described how unhealthy stress can be for your body and mind. As it turns out, anger can be even worse. In 2002, Johns Hopkins School of Medicine published a study in which they had tracked more than 1,000 medical students over 36 years.[48] Those who were prone to responding to stress with anger were three times more likely to develop heart disease and five times more likely to have had a heart attack by age 55. Further, other studies have demonstrated that in the hours following an intense bout of anger, your chances of experiencing a heart attack or stroke go up dramatically. When you're yelling at the parking attendant for misplacing your car keys, remember that it is you that will reap the consequences of that anger.

Anger Isn't Going To Help

"The best fighter is never angry." – Lao Tzu

One of the most important lessons one can ever learn is that anger is the least effective way to get what you want. Anger will never help the situation. Remember that when you're standing in line and it's taking forever or someone screws up your order. Yelling at the waitress isn't likely to get you your entrée any faster. Anger is even less likely to help if you're talking to someone you know well. Whether you're yelling at a coworker, or your spouse, or your sister, it will end badly. Charm is always a more effective way to get your desired result. In the next chapter, Kindness, you will find some tips on how to get your way without losing your temper.

You Can't Take It Back

"Beware of allowing a tactless word, rebuttal, a rejection to obliterate the whole sky." – Anaïs Nin

People say things in anger that they would never say ordinarily, things that hit below the belt. The problem is that you can never take it back. You might not have really meant that nasty thing you said to your spouse or your friend or your child. You might like to forget it ever happened, but I can assure you that the person you insulted never will. I'm sure you can think of examples in your own life where someone has said something to you in anger that you've never been able to forget. When arguments get heated they can get nasty. There are some things you don't ever want to say to those you care about most, and you put yourself at much greater risk of saying them when you're angry. Don't let fights get out of control. It's far too easy to make a mistake that you can't ever fix.

Adam and I have a rule where only one of us is allowed to be upset at a time. If one of us is really angry or frustrated, it becomes the job of the other to calm down the agitated person. It prevents situations from escalating. We were once trapped in an airport in Toronto for six hours with no food aside from some complimentary packets of cookies. And this was after having our flight canceled the previous day. I had reached the end of my rope. Adam wasn't too happy either, but he recognized that it was his job to keep me from totally losing it. The employees of that airline should be very grateful to him. Even when we're mad at each other, we still institute the rule. We know that fighting isn't going to solve anything. If one of us needs to vent occasionally, we don't take it personally and we don't retaliate. The focus should always be on finding solutions for problems rather than scoring points or placing blame.

It's Not About You

"Be kind, for everyone you meet is fighting a harder battle." –
Plato

It can be particularly difficult to remain calm when you
are interacting with someone who is angry at you, but it's still
worth it. It can be helpful to recognize that their anger almost
certainly has nothing to do with you. If someone is mad at you,
they probably just had a bad day or are in a bad mood. Or it
could be because whatever you've done hits too close to home.
When I got divorced people said some pretty nasty things to
me. They told me that I had made a commitment, and that I was
a terrible person for not following through with it. What I had to
realize was that most of that anger had nothing to do with me.
Yes, there were those who disagreed with what I was doing. In
fact, nearly everyone disagreed with what I was doing. I was
divorcing – and very much upsetting in the process – someone
they thought was a great guy. No one could understand why I
was doing it. There were those that didn't necessarily get it but
supported me anyway. And then there were those who were
really, really angry. Eventually I realized that the angriest of all
were those who were either afraid that their spouse would
leave them, or unhappily married unwilling to do anything
about it. They didn't want to hear why it was a good idea for me
to get divorced; they only wanted to yell as loud as they could
that getting divorced was a terrible, awful, selfish idea, no
matter what. They were yelling so loud because it was they who
needed convincing.

General Calm Gives Occasional Anger More Credence

"The right to be heard does not automatically include the right to be taken seriously." – Hubert Humphrey

Some people fly into a rage at the slightest provocation – a long line at the supermarket, heavy traffic, a delayed subway. Or they yell at their coworkers any time something goes wrong, or snap at their spouse for even the smallest indiscretion. If anger is your response to everything, people will find a way to tune you out. If they can avoid you completely, they will, and if they can't, they will stop listening. If you're angry all the time people will begin to attribute the anger to you, and think you are an angry person, rather than think whatever you're yelling about is actually a problem. The story of "the boy who cried wolf" is a classic for a reason: if you react to everything as though it's a crisis, there will be consequences.

Rather, when you are generally calm and composed, if you do on rare occasion get angry, people will sit up and listen. I was at my last job for five years. Over the course of that time, I built a reputation for being amiable and easy to work with. Which is why, on the one occasion in all that time I got into a heated argument with someone in the middle of a meeting, everyone rushed to take my side. It also helped that the man I was yelling at was thought of as unlikable and difficult – a reputation he earned by being regularly argumentative.

Anger Avoidance

"Anger is momentary madness, so control your passion or it will control you." – Horace

Once you're angry, it can be difficult to control. It's always a better idea to ward off anger before it starts.

Beware Anger Traps

I get cranky when I'm hungry. If I'm going to snap at my husband, it's going to be when I haven't eaten. We've joked that Adam should carry some food around with him at all times so he can shut me up quickly if necessary. Everyone has something that makes them particularly irritable. For some it's when they're tired. For others it's getting caught in traffic. If at all possible, avoid putting yourself in a situation in which you will be prone to anger. You obviously won't be able to avoid every source of annoyance, but you can eat regularly if hunger is your trigger, and you can get enough sleep if you are grumpy when you're tired.

Further, it's a good idea to give your partner some leeway when you know they're in a bad mood. Adam is always particularly tense when we travel. He hates airport security and customs and all the things that come along with it. He frequently gets angry with me during these moments, but I know it's just because he hates traveling and it makes him cranky. I don't take it personally. If you know there is a situation that's going to set your partner off, give them a wide berth and let it go.

Don't Let it Build

"Holding on to anger is like grasping a hot coal with the intent of throwing it at someone else; you are the one getting burned." – Buddha

Small problems have the ability to turn into big problems if they are left to fester. It's like wearing a pair of shoes that give you blisters. They will fine at first, and if you take them off or put on a Band-Aid soon enough, all will be well. But if you keep them on all day and walk for miles, the pain will become excruciating. You have to fix problems while they're fixable.

Unfortunately, I have quite a bit of experience with this. There have been far too many times in my own life when I've let something bother me for months if not years without actually doing anything about it. I work very hard at convincing myself there isn't a problem. I tell myself I'm overacting, or misinterpreting the situation, or that when push came to shove it wouldn't be an issue. But then one day some irrefutable bit of evidence lands in my lap and all that pent-up frustration explodes out at once, Armageddon style.

All of this more or less explains – though does not excuse – the hissy fit I threw at a recent street hockey game. I'm a wee bit touchy about my athletic abilities. Having played sports on co-ed teams as long as I have, I've endured my share of condescending attitudes about female athletes. I played on this touch football team once where every third play had to be a "girl play," i.e. had to directly involve one of the women on the team. The guys on the team always treated it like a wasted play, not believing the women could possibly have anything substantial to contribute. It became about mitigating the potential damage the women could cause rather than attempting anything productive. I sucked at football, so I didn't mind it as much as I might have. But I don't suck at hockey. In fact, I had the best season I ever had, scoring more goals than most of the men on my team. I thought it might have earned me a bit of respect. I thought it had, actually, which is where the denial came in. And then when the playoffs came around, and I still couldn't get anyone to pass me the ball, I completely lost it.

Clearly, a much better way of dealing with the situation would have been to address it ages ago when it started to bother me in the first place. Yelling and screaming was not going to help. It did not make anyone stop and think, "Gee, she has a good point." Rather, I think it made my teammates who had formerly liked and respected me start to question my sanity. I was able to salvage the situation eventually, but my tantrum did me more harm than good – and easily could have been avoided.

Assume Positive Intent
Everyone makes mistakes sometimes. A good way to prevent yourself from getting too angry too quickly is to assume positive intent. Everyone has a reason for doing what they have done and very rarely is that reason going to be, "to piss you off." Yes, there will be times when someone should have been more careful or responsible, and that can be frustrating. But there are many more effective ways to motivate someone to perform at their best than to yell at them when they screw up.

It is particularly important in romantic relationships to always, always assume that your partner didn't purposely try to upset you. If your husband didn't stop by the supermarket to buy milk like you asked, chances are it's not because he doesn't care about you but because he simply forgot. It's very tempting to say things like, "If you cared about me you wouldn't have forgotten. You know I need milk to make dinner. I'm cooking for you and you can't even bother to bring me what I need." You have to know, all the time, no matter what happens, that your partner is always going to do their best to be a good partner to you. If you aren't confident that that is the case, you have bigger problems than being without milk.

It's also really important to give someone a chance to explain before you get too worked up. It's always possible there is some extenuating circumstance you didn't know about. I worked for a woman who once had an employee that didn't show up for work for several days. No phone call, no email. She was furious. When the employee finally got in touch, it turned out that he had been in a coma in the hospital. Don't be angry until you give someone a chance to explain.

Wait It Out

It's always a good idea to take some time to cool off when you're going from an aggravating situation into a separate environment. All too many people are in the habit of getting angry at work or frustrated during their commute and then going home to take it out on their loved ones. Misdirected anger is the hardest kind to stomach if you're on the receiving end. It's bad enough to have someone be angry with you if you actually did something to upset them. Having someone give you a hard time when you had nothing to do with the problem in the first place is just downright unfair. If someone or something has made you really angry, take some time to calm down before dealing with anyone else.

Take a Moment

"If you are patient in one moment of anger, you will escape a hundred days of sorrow." – Rainer Maria Rilke

Because it is such a critical point, I would like to reiterate the importance of the relationship between anger and good luck. I cannot emphasize enough how imperative it is to control your temper. When something sets you off, *take a moment*. Take one moment to evaluate whether an emotional response is the one most likely to get you what you want. Take one moment to evaluate the possible damage you could do by reacting violently when you could chose to remain calm and composed. If you are someone prone to flying off the handle, you've likely convinced yourself that reacting in anger isn't a choice, and that there isn't a moment between an event and your response to it. But there is. There is always a moment. All that is required is the discipline to notice it. And if you need added motivation to look for that moment, please consider how much luckier it is likely to make you. Anger can be all that separates you from the life of your dreams. If you are upset about something at work and throw a fit about it, not only will you not get what you want, you could lose your job. If you are dating someone new and you lose your temper with them, it could be the end of that relationship. Anger will not have the effect you desire, and it will cause a lot of damage – often irreparable damage – in the process. So many people see those who regularly get what they want and think that it's all luck. It is not all luck. In difficult situations, composure and charm are what yield positive outcomes. If you are the one shooting yourself in the foot, you cannot blame your luck.

Caveat

Patience versus Inaction
"We must use time as a tool, not as a crutch." – John F. Kennedy

When you're "waiting for the universe to do its work," do everything you can do, and then stay relaxed and hopeful. Take action, and then wait. Do not use patience as an excuse to put off action. Don't waste time "waiting for the right moment." If you know what you want, go after it without hesitation. Hesitating out of fear is not strategic.

Don't (Always) Wait
There are times when you need to force the issue. There's a difference between being serene and being passive. If someone is toying with you, or leading you on, or dithering about a decision that affects your life, don't let them. Sometimes delays are inevitable, but if there is no good reason why you are being made to wait, don't wait.

False Serenity

Being serene doesn't mean that you should pretend not to be upset when you are, and being serene doesn't mean that you should let things slide or let people treat you in a way that isn't acceptable to you. You absolutely should stand up for yourself. I'd just like to make the point that there is a better way to do it then by throwing a tantrum. It's a lot easier to get someone to listen to your side of the story if you're not yelling.

Anger Has Its Place

"It's my rule never to lose my temper until it would be detrimental to keep it." – Sean O'Casey

Every now and then you will need to yell and scream. If something is time sensitive and you need to communicate the urgency – yell away. If you are dealing with someone who doesn't seem to hear you otherwise – yell away. Sometimes a few sharp words can save you a lot of time, or they will be the only way to get what you want. It's just important to remember that balance is key. No one will listen to what you're yelling if you yell all the time.

TENET #11: KINDNESS

"You know what charm is: a way of getting the answer yes without having asked any clear question." — Albert Camus, The Fall

When do people feel lucky? The answer to that question is simple: when they get what they want. And there is no easier way to get what you want than to be nice. As they say, "You get more flies with honey than you do with vinegar." We've all heard this expression since we were kids, yet how many of us really understand how powerful a concept it can be? Be nice for the sake of being nice, absolutely. But also know that being nice is the best possible way to get anything you want. Anything. Want people to like you? Be nice to them. Want people to think you're smart and talented and funny? Be nice to them. Want people to help you out? Be nice to them. Lucky people are well liked. You can be successful without people liking you, but it will be a lot more difficult – and a lot less enjoyable.

The Importance of Kindness

"It is absurd to divide people into good and bad. People are either charming or tedious." – Oscar Wilde, <u>Lady Windermere's Fan</u>

How much people like you matters more than just about anything. From your professional life to your personal life, the more likeable you are, the more successful you will be. The best explanation for why this is true comes from a concept in psychology known as the "halo effect." The halo effect refers to a phenomenon by which one characteristic of a person influences how people judge other, unrelated qualities of that person. That is, if they like you, they'll also think you're smart, and funny, and have all kinds of positive traits. Whereas if they think you're a jerk, they're more apt to think badly of you in other ways as well.

In one classic study of this effect conducted by Nisbett and Wilson in 1977, students were asked to view a recording of a college professor with a pronounced foreign accent teaching a class.[49] Half of the students watched a tape in which the professor was warm and engaging, and the other half saw this same professor behave in a cold and unfriendly manner. The students were then asked to rate the professor on his appearance, mannerisms and accent, qualities that should be totally unrelated to whether or not he was a nice guy. But the students who saw the tape of the professor behaving in a likable manner rated his appearance, mannerisms and accent much more highly than the students who saw the professor being a jerk. Further, the students were not aware that their feelings about the professor's likability had affected their ratings of these other factors. They didn't realize they'd judged his accent more harshly because he was obnoxious.

Another example of the halo effect in action is described by Malcolm Gladwell in his book *Blink*.[50] Believe it or not, how nice a doctor is to their patients is a much better predictor of whether they will be sued for malpractice than how good of a doctor they are. Mistakes happen in the medical profession all the time and most often patients never sue their doctors. But if a mistake occurs *and* the doctor didn't treat the patient with kindness and respect, a patient is much, much more likely to call their lawyer. The effect of a doctor's demeanor is so profound that a researcher found that she could predict whether a doctor had been sued for malpractice based solely on listening to ten-second long clips of interactions of that doctor with patients.[51] Bad doctors who are nice are less likely to be taken to court than great doctors who are rude.

When we like someone, we want to think highly of them. We see them in the best possible light and are forgiving of any foibles. But when we don't like someone, we look for any reason to confirm our conclusion that they're not a good guy. As I've said before, perception is reality. How much someone likes you dramatically affects their perception of you. In Confidence, I talked about looking the part. Now I'm suggesting that you look the part *and* be nice. If you can do those two things, you will give yourself the best possible chance to succeed.

The More (People) You Know

I used to hate the word "networking." It brought to mind slimy-looking guys in suits trying to force their business cards on people who didn't want them. And it seemed so disingenuous, like, "I'm only interested in meeting you because I think you might be able to help me." I wanted nothing to do with it. It wasn't until I read Max Gunther's book, *The Luck Factor*, that I realized I already had a network.[52] We all do – it's simply all of the people we know. And the more people we know, the luckier we are apt to be. As Gunther put it, our network is like a spider's web, and the bigger our web, the more likely we are to "catch" some good luck. Everyone is familiar with the phrase "It's not what you know, it's who you know." And the more people you know, the more likely you are to come across someone who can give you the lucky break you need. In many industries, it's not talent but connections that can get you to the top. You might be a fabulous actress but your path to success will be a lot smoother if you happen to know a casting agent. You could be a terrific lawyer but unless you know someone who is willing to give you a job, it won't matter.

When I realized what a critical role knowing a lot of people played in finding good luck, I stopped thinking of meeting new people as "networking" and starting thinking of it as making new friends. I had never befriended someone before because I thought they might help me, and I didn't intend to start. But I did go out of my way to make more lunch dates and invite more people for coffee runs. I volunteered for projects at work that I knew would bring me in contact with new people. I joined a book club and played on hockey teams where I didn't know anyone. It was a lot of fun and I made some great friends – legitimate friends, not people I was only hanging out with because I thought they could help me. People can tell if you're being sincere, and they'll know it if you're only looking for favors. You have to learn to love socializing. You'll create a vast network in the process, and there is no doubt that having more friends will enhance your life in other ways as well. Even if you never receive any tangible lucky breaks via friends – which is very unlikely – you'll never regret having more great people in your life.

Even making new casual acquaintances can prove to be beneficial. Someone doesn't have to be your best buddy to help you out. Sometimes good luck simply functions as a needs exchange: one party is looking for something, and the other party is the one who fits the bill. If you're looking to buy a car, and you meet someone who wants to sell their car, it can be lucky for you both. If you're looking for a new job and you come across someone who needs to hire someone new, you can both benefit. We've all seen this in action in the world of Facebook and Twitter. Someone you went to preschool with and haven't spoken to in twenty years could be your ticket to a free (gently used) sofa. Regularly people will post things like, "My friend is moving to New York next month, is anyone looking for a new roommate?" Between your own 600 friends, and all of your friend's friends, there is bound to be someone who has what you need.

To make the most of your network, you should let people know what you would consider to be good luck. The Facebook example is a simple one: if you're moving, ask your friends if anyone knows a great real estate agent. More broadly, though, you should get into the habit of talking about your goals. Describe your dream job, your dream home, your dream date. Your focus comes into play here – you have to know what you want before other people can know how to help you. And the more people you tell, the better chance you have of finding the help you need. It's a small world.

Charm 101

Even if they understand the importance of being well liked, many people simply don't know how to go about it. There are, fortunately, some simple steps you can take to ensure that just about everyone you meet will think you're a great guy or girl.

Talk About What They Like

There is nothing people enjoy more than talking about themselves and their favorite things. All you have to do is get them started and be genuinely interested in what they have to say. Ask them about their hobbies and then pay rapt attention as they detail the ins and outs of their stamp collection. Ask them about their days playing college basketball. Ask them why they decided to become a doctor. Ask them to tell you about their kids. People are happy when they're talking about something they love or a time in their life that was important to them. If people feel good when they're talking to you, they will associate that feeling with you. They will walk away thinking that you're a great guy or girl, when really, all you did was let them talk.

Get What They're Saying

Sincere interest and pointed questions will do in most situations, but a good way to score even more points is to have something intelligent to say about someone's topic of choice. For this reason, it pays to learn a little bit about as many subjects as possible. Follow current events, know enough about all of your city's major sports teams to be able to discuss them knowledgably, read a wide variety of books and familiarize yourself with popular TV shows. Some people you meet will want to talk about the recent election, and others are going to want to talk about Kim Kardashian's latest antics. Have something to say about either.

Follow Their Story

While you're listening to someone talk, try to remember what it is that they're telling you. People will find it enormously flattering if you can refer back to things that they've said to you in the past. People's stories are very important to them, and if you can remember the details, they'll feel that their stories are important to you as well. They'll believe that they must be special to have stood out in your memory.

First and foremost, remember their name. That's critical. And call them by their name so they know you remember it. Remember their kids' names, remember their spouse's name, remember what their interests are and what kind of work they do. Remember what is going on in their lives at the moment. Perhaps their daughter is applying to medical school, or they're planning a wedding. If you can inject a detail from a previous conversation into the current conversation, do so. Ask questions about things they've told you in the past. If someone tells you they're not feeling well, ask them how they're doing the next day. Keeping up with someone's story makes them feel as though you care about them, and it's nearly impossible not to like someone who genuinely cares about you.

Stay In Agreement

"Birds are taken with pipes that imitate their own voices, and men with those sayings that are most agreeable to their own opinions." – Samuel Butler

People tend to gravitate towards those who are the most like themselves. An easy way to instill a sense of familiarity – and increase the odds that someone is going to like you – is to agree with them. If they think the Red Sox manager is an idiot, agree that he's an idiot. If they think the new Batman movie is amazing, agree that it's amazing. When you first meet someone, it's not worth putting a wedge between you to disagree about whether or not it's going to rain tomorrow. Even a disagreement over the simplest thing can change someone's impression of you. If they think it's going to rain, agree that it's going to rain.

Another way in which we judge whether someone is like us or not is how they react to things. Some people are going to be thrilled when they walk past a Starbucks. They're going to want to run right in and get themselves a peppermint mocha. If you're with one of these people, get excited about Starbucks too. Other people hate Starbucks and will go well out of their way to find an independent coffee shop. If you're with one of these people, agree with them that it's worth the effort for a cozier feel. If you're walking around with your best friend, there's no need for you to pretend to like Starbucks if you don't. But if you're with someone who you don't know very well and who you want to like you, it's worth feigning some enthusiasm.

Make Them Feel Good

"The greatest good you can do for another is not just to share your riches, but to reveal to him his own." – Benjamin Disraeli

Everyone loves to be praised. If you compliment someone, they will like you. There is something to admire about anyone, and it will always pay to admire it. That is, it will always work to your favor so long as *the compliment is sincere.* A sincere compliment can work wonders, but an insincere one might backfire. If someone suspects you don't really believe what you're saying, they'll think you're just kissing up and are untrustworthy in general. Look for something that is legitimately praiseworthy, and praise it.

Further, when you praise someone, it always helps to go beyond the obvious. A classic example is telling a stunningly beautiful woman that she's smart, and telling a brilliantly intelligent woman that she's beautiful. Someone whose best quality is obvious is likely praised for it all the time. They will crave a kind word about some other feature that most aren't observant enough to notice.

Lastly, the best thing you can possibly compliment about anyone is something that they love about themselves. If I haven't already made it painfully obvious, I love that I'm a hockey player. It's my favorite thing about myself. If you tell me how awesome it is that I play hockey, or, even better, what a fantastic hockey player I am, I will most definitely like you!

Be a Friend

Beyond getting people to like you, there are a few extra steps you can take to turn new acquaintances into new friends.

Say Yes

A good friend of mine moved from London to New York a few years ago. At the time, she didn't know a single person in the city, and now she has a whole host of friends. I asked her once how she did it and she gave me a simple answer: "I said yes to every invitation I got." Every time a coworker she barely knew invited her to a barbeque, or a neighbor she just met invited her to a holiday party, she went. Some events were boring, or awkward, or she didn't meet anyone she liked. But there were those that turned out to be a great time and were full of interesting people who eventually became friends. Those of us who have lived in the same place for a long time and feel we already have plenty of friends are prone to turning down invitations to parties thrown by people we don't know very well. But we shouldn't; we never know who we're going to meet. I wasn't looking for new friends when I met Suzy, but now I'm so happy to have her in my life.

Be Fun

Why do we become friends with people in the first place? Because we have fun when we're with them. If an evening out with you is a good time, people are going to want to spend more evenings out with you. If, however, you're constantly complaining or dominating the conversation with long, boring stories, you're not going to get a lot of repeat invitations. We don't often consciously think to ourselves, "Is this person I'm out with having fun?" Instead, we're focused on whether or not we're having a good time, or we just go with the flow and don't think about it at all. But if you aren't paying attention to whether your potential new friend is having fun, you're leaving open the possibility that they're not.

Think about what the person you're spending time with would like to do. Just because you like posh cocktail bars doesn't mean they do. Maybe they prefer casual sports bars. Maybe they like French restaurants. A good friend takes that into account when suggesting a place to go out. Even better, allow them to choose the activity and location. Whatever they pick, go with it and be enthusiastic. Recall that similarity is something we look for in friends, and the easiest way to establish similarity is to agree to their suggestions. Of course, if they want to a sushi restaurant and you're allergic to seafood, it's appropriate to suggest something else. But, within reason, be as accommodating as possible. If you've let someone else choose someplace they like to go or an activity they enjoy doing, they're much more likely to have fun. There are those who prefer to have their activities planned for them. If you sense that is the case, go ahead and make some suggestions of your own. Come up with a range of options that would appeal to many tastes and allow them to pick among those.

It's particularly important in new relationships to make sure the other party enjoys your company, but even with established friendships, it's worth making the effort. If we've known someone for a long time, we tend to take it for granted that they have a good time when they're with us. Or worse, we no longer think that it matters if they have a good time. But it does. Have you every mysteriously lost touch with someone? Have you ever had a friend stop returning your calls or stop issuing invitations? It's possible that they've simply stopped enjoying your company. Everyone is entitled to an off day, or if you just faced some sort of personal crisis, of course you'll be dominating the conversation and you won't be overly positive. That's perfectly fine, but it's important to keep a balance. Again, if you are going through a tough time, people will understand. But the unfortunate truth is that even your best friends will eventually grow weary if you're no fun to be around.

Friendships are reciprocal arrangements. You always have to be giving as much – if not more – than you are getting. Make sure your friend's enjoyment is as important to you as your own. The more fun you are to be with, the more friends you will have and the more often they will want to see you.

Be Useful

Friends do things for one another. When you are an asset to someone, you give them an incentive to keep you around. If you're helping someone out, you can bet they're going to want to keep you a part of their life. Give someone a reason to be your friend. Lend them a book. Recommend a good restaurant. Help them move. Pick them up from the airport. For years, I've played on a number of hockey teams on which I'm the only woman. New York City can be a tough place to meet men, and I know a lot of men. Especially back when I was single, I felt that one thing I had to offer to my friends was access to a large pool of attractive, single men. I always had someone to come to parties with me because I always had invitations to parties where there would be plenty of guys. It was a perk of being my friend. Think about what perks you could be offering to the people in your life.

People will not only love you for helping them out in some way, but they'll also want to reciprocate. The need to reciprocate is a well-documented facet of human psychology. It's important not to expect or demand reciprocation; treat any favors you do as though they are gifts and don't expect anything in return. But if someone insists on returning the favor, let them. Once you start doing things for one another, your friendship will be cemented.

Listen and Understand

Sometimes the best thing a friend can do is sit back and listen. Many times when someone is upset or stressed or frustrated the only thing that will make them feel better is sharing their troubles with someone else. At times like this, it's best to just let them get it out. They want to be heard, they want to be reassured, and they want to be comforted. It is not the time to problem-solve, and it's certainly not the time to tell them how you think they contributed to the situation. Even if you believe your friend is the one at fault or that they have no reason to be upset, just listen. It doesn't matter if their feelings are rational or not. The emotions they are experiencing are real, and they want someone to hear them out.

Further, human beings all have the basic need to be understood. When someone tells you they are upset, they want you to understand *why* they are upset. When your friend is venting, pay close attention, and if you need to, ask clarifying questions. When they're finished telling their story, demonstrate that you've understood what they've told you. A classic technique that therapists use is restating the story. You can say something like, "So, your boss yelled at you in front of everyone even though you had nothing to do with the problem?" Once you're sure that you understand – and *they're* sure that you understand – empathize with their emotions. Say things like, "I can see why you're upset," or "Anyone would be frustrated in your situation," or "I'd be angry too if someone said that to me." It makes the person who is upset feel they have been heard and that their feelings have been validated.

Lastly, it's important to use some of the techniques I discussed in Awareness. In addition to hearing their words, try to understand what their body language is telling you. Sometimes someone won't come out and say that they're upset, but if you pay attention you'll be able to see it on their face or in their tone of voice. When you can see what someone is feeling without their having to tell you, you'll have a friend for life.

Friendly Beliefs

When you're meeting someone new, perhaps the most important thing you can do is assume that the other person will like you. Numerous studies have demonstrated that if you are under the impression that someone likes you, you will behave in a way that actually results in that person liking you. And the opposite is true as well – if you believe that someone does not like you, you are likely to say and do things that will cause the other person to not like you.

A study conducted in 1986 by Rebecca Curtis and Kim Miller examined what factors lead to this self-fulfilling prophecy (or "expectancy confirmation", as it's described in the research).[53] As it turns out, many of the factors are those I've mentioned before. Participants who believed they were liked disagreed less frequently, were generally more positive, and disclosed more about themselves. Earlier in the chapter I discussed how getting people to talk about themselves would lead them to like you; the authors of this study suggested that disclosing things about yourself is a way you can get others to disclose things about themselves. The disclosure becomes reciprocal. I also suggested that agreeing with someone – and avoiding disagreement – is another means by which to make someone like you. Curtis and Miller's research supports this, and demonstrated a positive correlation between agreement and liking. Lastly, the research demonstrates that those with a positive demeanor were more likable. As I suggested in the chapter on Happiness, people like happy people. A sunny disposition makes people want to be around you.

What's so interesting about this research, though, is not just that it confirms some of the factors that would make someone like you, but that it implies that when you assume people like you, you *automatically* do these things. When you believe someone likes you, you naturally behave in a way that leads to that outcome. You won't even have to think about getting someone to talk about themselves and agreeing more and being upbeat. It would just happen. It suggests that believing that people like you is an easy place to start if you're hoping to increase your general likability.

Further, in addition to making new friends, having friendly beliefs can also make you more successful. In her book, *How to Be a People Magnet*, Leil Lowndes describes a University of Pennsylvania study in which life insurance salesmen were given a "personality survey," which addressed, among other things, whether they generally believed that people will like them.[54] In the months following the survey, the ones who believed that people will like them sold 37% more insurance than those who didn't. Can't argue with that.

Avoid Conflict

"If they want peace, nations should avoid the pinpricks that precede cannon shots." – Napoleon Bonaparte

It's a lot easier to get people to like you if you can avoid making them angry, or, if you do make them angry, if you can quickly resolve the situation. Follow these suggestions to avoid getting in your own way.

Be Diplomatic

Everyone has strong opinions about some things. When you first meet someone, however, it's best to keep those opinions to yourself. If you can, avoid saying things like, "I hate people who…." Or "It drives me crazy when people…." There is always the chance that the person you've just met does one of those things. You probably won't even know you've offended them, and then you'll be surprised when they don't return your phone call. Or, you put someone in the embarrassing position of having to admit to the behavior or attribute you've just ridiculed. Being a graduate of the Wharton School of Business, this has happened to me a lot. Let's just say that Wharton students don't have a reputation for being the nicest of people. I can't tell you how many times someone has made a comment to me about what assholes they think people who went to Wharton are. Obviously, they had no idea I went there when they said it, but it doesn't make the situation less awkward when I point out that they're talking about me. If you're not careful, it's very easy to unintentionally insult someone, and it can be a difficult situation to smooth over. It's really hard to take back a statement that you *just made*. Be careful about making strong opinions known, especially in a professional setting. It's like how they say you should never talk about politics or religion on a first date. Don't run the risk of offending someone before they've had a chance to get to know you.

Be Fair

In their book *Sway*, authors Ori and Rom Brafman talk about a concept known as procedural justice.[55] According to this concept, people will be more upset by a process they view as being unfair than by a poor outcome. The authors described a survey of car dealers that examined the dealers' feelings on their interactions with car manufacturers.[56] They note that while one doesn't ordinarily think of car dealers as slaves to "fairness," it's actually quite important to them. Generally, car dealers are at the mercy of car manufacturers and have little control over their own inventory and pricing. The results of the survey indicated that the dealers were less concerned with the outcomes of their interactions, i.e. the cost of the cars they were getting and the models they were required to buy, and more concerned with whether or not they felt the car manufacturers treated them with respect and took the time to understand the dealers' particular market and concerns. They didn't mind getting stuck with bad inventory if they felt the process was fair.

The lesson here is that even if you have to give someone bad news or tell them something they don't want to hear, they will be much more receptive if they feel they have been treated fairly and that you care about their individual concerns. Everyone is much more able to deal with disappointment if they believe the process that led to the disappointment was a fair one. If you tell me I have to come to work on a Saturday for a project that isn't urgent and that no one else is going to be required to come in, I'm going to be upset. But if you explain to me why it's so important and that you yourself will be coming in as well, I won't mind so much. People don't like being taken advantage of. I'm never going to enjoy working on a Saturday, but if I feel the request is fair, I won't be angry about it.

Disarm

Some people are just difficult to deal with. They have prickly personalities and get offended very easily. If someone is upset with you, there are some simple things you can do to bring them back into the fold. First, as I mentioned in Serenity, calm is contagious. Remaining calm can go a long way towards soothing someone who is upset. Second, the easiest way to quickly shut down anyone who is angry with you is to agree with them. Even if they are being wildly irrational, say something like, "Yes, you're totally right, I can see why you're angry." If you're not fighting against them, they have no reason to keep arguing. It takes the fight right out of them. Oftentimes, they'll even see the error in their own argument. People always become more rational when they are calm and feel understood.

A Good Influence

"Don't raise your voice, improve your argument." – Desmond Tutu

We tend to think of "influence" as the power to get someone to do what we want. The means by which most people "influence" others is by making demands, yelling at them, punishing them, or forcing their hand in one way or another. As I mentioned in the previous chapter, Serenity, this isn't a good strategy. A much more effective way to influence people is to make them to *want to do* what you want them to do. If you can learn to influence in this way, you can get more of what you want – and in the process make friends rather than enemies. You can get those that work for you to do a better job, and get them to like you at the same time. Learning to influence in the right way can feel like a miracle.

Ask Nicely

This should go without saying, but I'd be remiss if I didn't mention it: it really does pay to ask nicely. It doesn't matter if someone is getting paid to make you that cup of coffee. Ask nicely. It doesn't matter that it's your secretary's job to type up that report. Ask nicely. It doesn't matter if it's your husband's turn to go to the supermarket. Ask nicely. It makes the difference between whether someone happily fulfills your request – and does it to the best of their ability – or grudgingly complies and expends as little effort as possible.

Even if you have to ask for someone to fix something they screwed up in the first place, ask nicely. It can be incredibly tempting to snap at someone who has just screwed up your order or lost your reservation. But remember that your ultimate goal is to get what you want as quickly as possible. If you want your eggs scrambled and not sunny-side up, ask nicely: "I'm sorry sir, I hate to be a bother, but I had asked for these eggs to be scrambled." If the hotel loses your reservation, you can either berate the desk clerk – who probably had nothing to do with the screw-up – or you can actually try to get what you want. You are always much more likely to get what you want if you ask nicely.

Reward Rather than Punish

"The consequences of an act occurring affect the probability of its occurring again." – B.F. Skinner

B.F. Skinner was a pioneer in the field of learning theory. As part of his research, he explored the role played by enforcement in teaching new skills and behaviors. He was of the opinion that positive reinforcement was much more effective than negative reinforcement. He felt that rather than punish poor behaviors, one should wait for the student to exhibit the desired behavior and then to reward it. He believed negative reinforcement led one to dislike and avoid the very activity the teacher was trying to teach. Rather, if training could be seen as something positive that might lead to reward, a student would enjoy learning. Skinner utilized animal training studies to demonstrate that positive learning techniques did in fact lead animals to learn more quickly and retain the information longer.

Amy Sutherland's book, *What Shamu Taught Me About Life, Love and Marriage*, which I first discussed in the section on Responsibility, adapts these concepts for humans.[57] She points out that we are constantly reinforcing the behaviors of those around us, whether we realize it or not. In that section, I discussed the way in which reinforcement affects our relationships and the way people treat us. For example, if you don't take the bait when your sister-in-law tries to pick a fight, eventually she'll stop trying to pick fights. You can take the same concepts a step further and use them to encourage or discourage any behavior you'd like. If you have an employee who is always late for work, rather than punishing them for being late, you can give them an incentive to be on time. Or if you want your daughter to keep her room clean, you can praise and reward her when she does manage to tidy up. It's always more effective to be positive. Further, the more negative reinforcement you dish out, in the form of criticism, yelling, and punishment, the less likely it is that the person you're trying to influence is going to like you. As I hoped I've convinced you, being liked is important, and it will always make it more likely that someone is going to do what you want.

Set Them Up For Success

Another concept Skinner felt was critical to learning was giving the student the chance to succeed. When you want someone to do something for you, it is your responsibility to make sure they are able to accomplish the task.

First and foremost, make sure it's clear to them what you want. If your instructions are vague, and you don't wind up getting exactly what you wanted, you can't blame the other party for failing to execute. Only clear parameters can get clear results. You can't fault people for not being able to read your mind.

Further, make sure the other party has what they need to accomplish the task. Do they have the necessary training? Do they have the resources they require? Do they have enough time to accomplish the task? It's not fair to ask someone to do something without ensuring a reasonable path to success.

I've talked before about my awful job in advertising. I was in the unfortunate position of taking over for someone who had been doing my job for three years. She was great at her job, and the company loved her. That wasn't the problem. The problem was that they kept expecting me to be her – along with her three years of experience. They were chronically frustrated with me for not being immediately up to speed with what it took the woman I replaced years to master. My favorite example of this was the Chicago Marathon debacle. One of our clients was a sponsor of the Chicago marathon. When I interviewed for the job, they went on about how well my predecessor had done managing this campaign. In addition to their praise for her, they noted (repeatedly) that they had only given her the responsibility of managing the project because she had been doing the job for several years and had earned the opportunity. They emphasized that if I too did a great job for the next couple years, I could expect the same opportunity. Meanwhile, a few months later, they were furious with me when they learned that I had not been preparing for the marathon campaign. This was despite the fact that they *had not asked me to do so* and, again, had told me my predecessor was only asked to do so because of her years of experience. It was maddening.

What I found most frustrating about that position was that I felt like I couldn't win. I didn't get anywhere near the kind of training I needed to do my job, and then I was criticized when

I couldn't do my job. When someone gets the impression that they are being set up to fail, they will not be motivated. When someone begins to feel that there is no way they could possibly succeed, they will give up trying. When you want something done, make sure you give the person you're asking the best chance to get it done.

Inspire Desire

"...the only way on earth to influence other people is to talk about what they want and show them how to get it." – Dale Carnegie, How to Win Friends and Influence People

Like it or not, people will generally not do things just because you want them to. People are only motivated to do the things they want to do. If you present something to someone, stated in the terms of what you want and why it will be good for you, they're not going to be very motivated. And if you force them into it in one way or another, you're not going to get the results you're looking for. No one does their best work when it feels like what they're doing is an obligation. If, however, you state what you want in terms of why it will benefit them, you might find them motivated after all.

Sometimes providing a reward is the way to go. If you want your husband to wash the car or fix the doorbell, you might find your request falling on deaf ears. But if you state it in terms he can understand, say, "If you wash the car we can go see the new action movie tonight instead of the chick flick I'd much rather see," you might find him complying.

If a reward isn't appropriate, you can often find a reason why it is in a person's best interests to do something.

This strategy can be even more effective. For example, research demonstrates that it's much better to get kids to want to do well in school rather than to reward them for good grades. If they're only doing their homework to get a reward, the homework will stop when the rewards stop. If, however, you can help them to understand why achieving in school would be so advantageous for them, you might find them doing their homework without complaint. Take them on tours of some good colleges and get them thinking about future careers. Show them how much they stand to benefit from their hard work.

If you're negotiating in business, you have to present the deal in a way that demonstrates to the other party why it is the best deal for them. When you apply for jobs, you have to tell your potential employers why you would be an asset to the company, not why you want the job. People don't care what's in it for you. They only want to know what's in it for them.

Encourage

Never underestimate the value of encouragement. I've discussed the importance of providing a reward, and sometimes the best kind of reward is praise. It's important not to save up your praise until the project is done, but to dole some out along the way. If someone is learning something new, they might not be very good at it at first. It can be frustrating and make that person want to give up. Having a little encouragement can make all the difference.

Even when someone is appropriately motivated, some encouragement does not go amiss. I know when I was writing this book, I needed all I could get. Writing it was a long, arduous process. Even though I enjoyed what I was doing, and even though I was excited about the book, the encouragement is what kept me going. My husband and friends were wonderful at keeping me motivated and focused. They also kept me feeling good about what I was doing. They believed in me and told me so along the way. Not once or twice, but regularly. It made all the difference between having a finished product and a perpetual work in progress.

Aim High (For Them)

"It is the nature of man to rise to greatness if greatness is expected of him." – John Steinbeck

In Dale Carnegie's classic *How to Win Friends and Influence People*, one of his recommendations is to give someone a "reputation to live up to."[58] He felt people tend to rise to the level of expectation that you set for them. If you expect someone to do a great job, they'll often prove you right. But if you expect someone to screw up, don't be surprised when they do. People want to feel good about themselves. It's a bonus if you can make someone feel good about him or herself before they've done anything. If you tell someone you believe they will succeed, you are giving them an extraordinary incentive. It makes them want to do the thing they were praised for. Simple phrases like, "I know that you're going to do a great job on that report" or "I know you're going to play really well in your game," can have a profound effect. As many things do, it goes back to Belief. What you are doing is giving someone a reason to believe in themselves. And, alternatively, if you give someone a reason to believe they aren't going to succeed, they'll believe that as well. For both yourself and others, what you believe tends to be what you achieve.

Kindness is a Lifestyle

"The true measure of a man is how he treats someone who can do him absolutely no good." – Samuel Johnson

As I hope I've conveyed, being nice to people can help you to get what you want. It can help you make friends and it can motivate people to help you out. It can even prevent you from being sued for malpractice. But getting something in return is not the only reason to be nice to people. Be nice just for the sake of being nice.

First of all, whether or not you realize it, people will notice how you treat others. Even if you're really nice to your date, she's going to notice how you treated the waitress. Even if you're very polite to your mother-in-law, she's going to notice how you treated the taxi driver. If people see you being rude to someone else, they're going to think you might treat them that way someday as well. My boss at my last job was always exceptionally nice to me. He nominated me for a prestigious leadership training course, and I know he sang my praises around the company. It made me uncomfortable, though, when I saw how he treated some of my co-workers. I did a good job, and I deserved to be treated well, but so did the colleagues of mine who regularly felt the wrath of his infamous temper. I'm of the opinion that no matter how poor someone's job performance is, they always deserve to be treated with respect. I had a few reasons for leaving that position, but pretty high on the list was not wanting to work for someone who could be unkind, even if he was never unkind to me.

Obviously, there are good reasons to be nice when someone else can see you. But even if no one is watching, even if you're not with a friend, or a date, or a co-worker, you should still be nice to people. Make kindness a habit. If it's not something you do all the time, it's really easy to "slip" when it matters. You might forget your manners when you're on a first date and the bartender spills your drink, or over lunch with your boss when the waitress brings you the wrong sandwich. When kindness is something you just turn on from time to time, it could shut off at an inconvenient moment. If it's something you do all the time, it never fails you. Not to mention that being nice is just the right thing to do.

Love the Ones You Love

"It is not a lack of love, but a lack of friendship that makes unhappy marriages." – Friedrich Nietzsche

It's important to be nice to people. But it's really, really important to be nice to the people you love. Sounds obvious, I know, but many people fall into the habit of treating their nearest and dearest with less kindness than they would treat a stranger. There are those who think they don't have to be polite to friends and family, believing that it's no longer necessary. Something I'm really proud of in my relationship with Adam is how kind we are to one another. We make an effort to do the little things. We always say please and thank you. We always speak to each other respectfully, even when we disagree. We always ask nicely when we want something, and if we're asked for something, we happily comply. Adam has never been one for grand romantic gestures. If I wanted a surprise trip to Tahiti for my birthday I would have been disappointed. But what Adam is amazing at is "treating me like a princess" each and every day. Anyone can send flowers on occasion, but it takes real effort to show kindness to your spouse *all the time*. It means making sure you always have their favorite flavor of ice cream in the freezer. It means going out to your spouse's favorite restaurant even if you would have rather stayed in. It means calling your spouse if you're going to be home late. It means not complaining about being woken up at 7am on a Saturday to watch soccer (yet again). And it means not getting angry when one of you forgets to do the laundry or breaks your favorite mug.

There is a great song by Natalia Kills called "Love is a Suicide." There's a line in the song that says, "You love me like an enemy." I think I used to love like an enemy. I treated the men I was interested in like adversaries, as though we were on opposing sides in a war and there would only be one winner. I wanted the power, I wanted the control, and I always wanted to come out ahead. I wanted to win, not to love. True love isn't about keeping score. True love is about giving, not receiving. Find joy in giving to your spouse, to your friends, and to your family. If you're giving time, love, and affection to someone with the expectation that they will give it in return, you are setting yourself up for disappointment. Put all your energy into making your spouse happy because you love them and for no other reason. Have the happiness of others be what makes you happy.

Caveat

Know the Difference Between Charm and Sleaze

Charm loses all its power if people know that you're trying to "charm" them. Charm isn't about pretending to be kind and engaging; charm is about being genuinely kind and engaging. Trying to fake it will backfire.

You Can't Always Agree

Agreeing with someone you first meet about their opinion on the new Coldplay album is a good idea. Agreeing with everything they say every time you see them is a bad idea. Agreement is important to establishing an initial rapport, but it isn't necessary – or advisable – to keep up the agreement forever. Nor is it a good idea to pretend to be someone you're not. If you pretend to love skiing on a first date don't be surprised if you find yourself honeymooning in Aspen. Better to politely suggest that, while skiing is great, you're really more of a beach person.

Preemptive Unkindness

There will be times when it's necessary to make it clear right away that you are not to be messed with. If someone you've just met challenges your authority or position, it's best to dress them down quickly. The situation will only escalate if you don't send the right signals from the start. I found myself in this position a few times when Adam and I first started dating.

There were a couple of women he knew who obviously felt they had already staked a claim on him. When some rude comments were made to me, my reaction let them know that going down that road would be a poor decision. Don't let people toy with you.

Don't Let People Take Advantage

If you're being nice, and someone isn't being nice back, stop being nice. If those around you are taking and taking and not giving, walk away. Friendships are reciprocal relationships. That means that if you are not getting anything out of it, they should not be your friend. You can't be the only one doing the giving.

Don't Be a Mommy (or Daddy) Martyr

"Nothing has a stronger influence psychologically on their environment and especially on their children than the unlived life of the parent." – C.G. Jung

I've mentioned before how much I love the TV show *What Not to Wear*. Just about every mother who goes on that show talks about how uncomfortable she feels focusing on herself and how she always puts everyone else first. So many women fall into the trap of thinking of themselves as wives and mothers and nothing else. The happiness of their family comes before their own. No matter how many kids you have, your own happiness matters, and you can't take care of anyone if you don't take care of yourself first. There is nothing wrong with wanting your kids to have a better life than you've had, or taking joy in making them happy. Those are wonderful instincts to have. But the happiness of your family can't come at the *expense* of your own. I'm certain that you want your happy kid to one day become a happy adult. The best way to ensure that is to provide a good example.

TENET # 12: GRATITUDE

"Many people who order their lives rightly in all other ways are kept in poverty by their lack of gratitude." – Wallace Wattles

A critical component to becoming a luckier person is *feeling* like a luckier person. It may sound obvious, but it's true. It doesn't matter how many good things happen to you in your life if you can't appreciate them. If you take the good things for granted, you'll never feel good. You have to notice your good luck in order to feel lucky. Further, feeling lucky can even bring you more good luck. As the incomparable Oprah Winfrey once put it, "Be thankful for what you have; you'll end up having more. If you concentrate on what you don't have, you will never, ever have enough."

The Power of Gratitude

"A thankful heart is not only the greatest virtue, but the parent of all other virtues." - Cicero

In recent years, researchers have begun to examine the effect that gratitude has on our lives, and, as it turns out, its effect is profound. Being grateful can lead to a surprising abundance of positive outcomes. In 2010, Dr. Alex Wood and colleagues published a review article outlining all of the research that had been done on gratitude to date.[59] Here is an overview of their findings:

- Grateful people are happier.
- Grateful people are less angry and hostile.
- Gratitude is associated with the kinds of characteristics that lead one to be socially successful, such as emotional warmth, gregariousness, activity seeking, trust, altruism, and tender-mindedness.
- Grateful people are less likely to suffer from psychiatric disorders. In one large study, "thankfulness" was associated with a lower risk of major depression, generalized anxiety disorder, phobia, nicotine dependence, alcohol dependence, drug abuse or dependence and bulimia nervosa.
- Gratitude has been shown to be helpful to those who have experienced a traumatic event. Those who were able to take something positive away from the experience were able to recover more quickly. Many even experienced greater overall well-being after the event,

feeling that they had developed a better appreciation of life and the importance of family and friends.

- Gratitude is associated with better relationships. Interestingly, several studies have surveyed the friends and family of those participating in a gratitude study, and these studies demonstrated that the friends and family also benefit when an individual feels more gratitude. Gratitude may help people to feel more connected, "increase reciprocally helpful behavior," and "promote conflict resolution."

- The relationship between gratitude and health is not as clear. There has, however, been some evidence suggesting that gratitude can reduce stress. Given all the negative health implications of stress, gratitude could improve health in that way. Further, gratitude has been shown to have a positive influence on sleep.

If you are already routinely grateful for the good things in your life, congratulations. You are likely enjoying at least some of the positive benefits outlined above. If, however, you're looking to inject a bit of gratitude into your life, it might be easier than you think. One of the pioneers of gratitude research, Dr. Robert Emmons, wrote a book called *Thanks!*, in which he describes the results of the studies he has conducted over the years.[60] Emmons was the first to test whether becoming grateful could induce some of these positive effects. In his initial study, he randomly assigned participants to one of three groups.[61] The first group was asked to write down five things they were grateful for that had occurred in the previous week. They were asked to do this once a week for ten weeks. Another group was asked to write down five bad things that had happened over the week, and the final group was asked to write down five observations of their week, regardless of whether they were positive or negative. After ten weeks, those in the gratitude group were a full 25% happier than the other two groups. Those in the gratitude group also reported having fewer health complaints and even exercised more on average than the other groups. They wrote down five sentences once a week and became demonstrably happier and healthier. That's an amazing reward for such a small amount of effort. In subsequent studies, Dr. Emmons upped the frequency and had people make their gratitude lists every day and found the positive effects to be even stronger. No one can claim they don't have time to write down five sentences once a week. And if you can feel grateful more often than that, all the better.

Routinely Grateful

"We can only be said to be alive in those moments when our hearts are conscious of our treasures." – Thornton Wilder

As you can see, being regularly grateful has many advantages. And the easiest way to make gratitude a bigger part of your life is to make it a habit. In the chapter on Persistence, I described the necessary components to creating a habit: a cue, a routine, and a reward. My personal gratitude habit is thinking about five things that I'm thankful for right before I fall asleep at night. The cue is getting into bed, the routine is thinking of the five things, and the reward is the happy feeling I get when I remind myself of the good things in my life. Every night I start with the same one: I'm grateful for my husband, Adam. I know that it's all too easy to take your partner for granted, so I make it a point to be thankful for him every day. From there I let my imagination run wild. I'll be thankful for my amazing girlfriends if I've just spent a night having dinner with them. I'll be thankful for my hockey team if we've just won a game (or had a great time at the bar afterwards). I'll be thankful for the weather if it was a nice day, or I'll be thankful for a TV marathon of *America's Next Top Model* if it wasn't. Sometimes I'm thankful for the critical-but-boring things like my health and having enough food to eat. Other times I'm thankful for the little things that aren't critical at all, like a great glass of wine or a new book by my favorite author. Another regular item on the list is gratitude for having the chance to follow my dream. And then I'm grateful in advance for the day my dream comes true!

When you develop your own gratitude ritual, think about what would make the most sense for your lifestyle. The ritual doesn't have to happen every day, but it should be done at least once a week. It's more important that you enjoy your gratitude ritual than that you do it daily. If the ritual starts to feel like a chore, it won't give you the happy feeling you're looking for.

So Much to be Grateful For

"If you want to make an apple pie from scratch, you must first invent the universe." – Carl Sagan

In his book *Thanks!*, Dr. Robert Emmons provides his own definition of gratitude.[62] He believes gratitude consists of two factors. The first part is an acknowledgment of something positive. That is, to feel gratitude, you first have to recognize that there is something to be grateful *for*. The second part of gratitude is the awareness that the source of this good thing is someone or something outside of yourself. For example, a friend did you a favor, your boss gives you the afternoon off, or the weather was beautiful on the day of your outdoor wedding. Dr. Emmons goes on to say that part of what makes gratitude tricky for some is that it requires them to acknowledge that they are not the sole source of the good things in their lives. As he puts it, "Gratitude implies humility – a recognition that we could not be who we are or where we are in life without the contribution of others." It can be difficult to give credit to others, particularly if you've had to work very hard to achieve what you have. But very rarely will someone become successful without some form of help along the way.

I think the above quote by Carl Sagan is an excellent way to illustrate this idea. Everything we want to create for ourselves depends upon an endless array of things that we had nothing to do with. I might want credit for baking that pie, but I didn't plant the apple trees. I didn't pick the apples. I didn't mill the wheat to make the flour. I didn't grow sugarcane and process it into the two cups of sugar I needed. I didn't milk the cows, and I didn't turn that milk into butter. I didn't drive the truck that transported those products to the supermarket. I don't own the supermarket that gathered these items and I didn't stock the shelves. All I can be credited for is the trip to the store and a couple hours of baking. Sure, there would be no pie if I hadn't baked it, but I couldn't have baked it without the efforts of countless other individuals. I know that farmers didn't grow those apples solely for my benefit, and I know the supermarket doesn't exist just so that I might bake. But it doesn't mean I can't be grateful to them for providing me with what I need.

Many people feel they need not be grateful for their success because they believe they have earned it. It's perfectly reasonable to congratulate yourself for all of your hard work, but your hard work does not mean that there is nothing to be grateful for. Professional athletes have to work really, really hard to be successful, but no basketball player can take credit for being seven feet tall. We're all born with certain strengths, and we all have to work really hard to hone those strengths if we want to make anything of ourselves. But we should still be thankful for the strengths we were born with.

Another thing I find lacking from the "I earned this" argument is that much of the course our life is determined before we're old enough to make any decisions for ourselves. Much of my husband's life now is shaped by the fact that he played hockey when he was a kid. Adam started playing hockey when he was seven years old. He might have been the one skating around, but Adam wasn't driving himself to practice. Adam wasn't buying his own equipment. He wasn't taking himself to the doctor when he got injured. Adam was lucky and had amazing parents who did everything they could to support and encourage him. There are kids, however, whose parents don't support them. This could be due to financial hardship, or a culture that doesn't place a high value on extracurricular activities for children, but there are some kids who don't get to play sports, or learn instruments, or take dance classes, or do any of the things that might give them a leg up on their classmates. Because Adam played hockey, he was recruited by an elite high school, which in turn allowed him to get into a good college, and then to get a good job. Adam himself had to work hard both at his sport and in school to make the most of his opportunities. But that doesn't mean he shouldn't be grateful for them. Some kids don't get the same chances, through no fault of their own.

No matter how hard we work to get what we have, we all owe our success in part to outside factors. It does not make our own achievements any less impressive if we express gratitude for them. It doesn't matter who or what you are grateful to. Many people thank God or some other religious entity for their good fortune. If you are one of those people, go right ahead. But if you are not religious, it doesn't mean you can't be grateful. Gratitude puts our achievements in perspective. Gratitude encourages us to pay it forward. And gratitude keeps us humble. The most successful among us aren't those who have done everything for themselves. They are the ones who made the most of the help they have received. When you get the good luck you're looking for, say thank you.

A Matter of Perspective

"Remember, remember, this is now, and now, and now. Live it, feel it, cling to it. I want to become acutely aware of all I've taken for granted." – Sylvia Plath

Adam and I have a phrase we like to say whenever we find ourselves getting upset over something trivial: "first world problems." Once again, as discussed in the Happiness section, we tend to get used to our environments pretty quickly, no matter how good they are. We evaluate problems that arise relative to the general state of our lives. It's the classic "poor little rich kid" scenario: a child is so used to getting everything he wants that he throws a tantrum when he is denied even the smallest thing. Meanwhile, in some parts of the world, there are still children who are sold into slavery. We get so used to the quiet comfort of our lives that we no longer find ourselves being grateful for the quiet and comfort.

Here in New York, we were all recently affected by hurricane Sandy, which resulted in more than a hundred deaths, thousands of destroyed homes, and left hundreds of thousands without power. Tragic events like this one shift the scale with which we judge our luck. If you lived in New York or New Jersey and nothing at all bad happened to you, you would be considered to be extremely lucky, even if your life was exactly the same as it was before the storm. Luck is always a matter a perspective. As horrible as events like the recent storm are, they at least have the effect of showing us the kind of perspective we should always have, i.e., "I have running water, electricity, and a roof over my head, so I am a lucky, lucky girl." For most of us, our ordinary, everyday lives do make us really, really lucky. It's just that the ordinary everydayness of it all tends to make us forget it.

In the days following the hurricane, I heard the same kinds of stories that everyone in the region heard, about people who lost their homes and about neighborhoods that were destroyed. I also heard countless unlucky-but-not-quite-as-unlucky stories about people who were without power and had to walk up and down the 29 floors to their apartment, people living in areas where the water had been contaminated, and people whose commutes lasted for hours while the subway was shut down. These second tier bad luck stories would ordinarily make anyone frustrated and annoyed and feel rather unlucky.

Sitting in four hours of traffic is always going to suck, but in times like these, our *perspective* on the traffic changes. We begin to think, "It may suck to be stuck here, but at least we didn't lose our car to the flood waters like so-and-so."

This perspective game, the "In what way does this make me lucky?" game, can be a lot harder to play when you've experienced a truly devastating event. But it's still not impossible. Over the course of our lives, at one time or another, we will likely all be the victims of some terrible luck. If the terrible luck is something that it's at least possible to recover from, that is one thing to be grateful for. If something or someone is lost forever, it can be more difficult, but you can always be grateful for time you had together. As mentioned earlier in the chapter, research has indicated that if you can find something to be grateful for, it's possible to recover more quickly. It's even possible to gain a greater appreciation for life.

The perspective game is also a lot easier to play in times of crisis when it's obvious that there are others suffering more than we are. But the unfortunate truth is that there is always a crisis somewhere. It's so easy to forget, since most of us don't live in Afghanistan, or Darfur, or Haiti. We don't usually feel lucky just because we have a functioning sewer system. But we should. I'm just as guilty as anyone of getting cranky when the DVR doesn't record my favorite show or Trader Joe's runs out of the frozen spanakopita triangles I like so much. But I'm learning to put my disappointments in perspective.

Appreciation

"They do not love that do not show their love." – William Shakespeare

Appreciation can enhance every relationship in your life, but there is no relationship where it is more important than in your marriage. Expressing gratitude to your spouse can save you from divorce. Dr. John Gray, a leading couple's counselor, wrote a book called *The Truth About Cheating*.[63] Seeing the devastation that infidelity can cause in a relationship, he began to investigate the causes of cheating. He felt that if he could better understand what leads to cheating, he could recommend ways of preventing it. He surveyed and interviewed thousands of men who had cheated on their wives and asked them why they did it. (Obviously, men are not the only ones that cheat in relationships, but men were the focus of his studies. I think much of what he found is applicable to women as well.) Unsurprisingly, Dr. Gray found that the most common factor leading to whether a man would cheat is dissatisfaction with the marriage. What was surprising, however, was that in the grand majority of cases, it was emotional rather than sexual dissatisfaction that led to the cheating. Our society tends to give us the idea that men are depraved creatures who only think about sex and thus it's hardly surprising that many men cheat. In reality, however, most of the men that Dr. Gray surveyed strayed from their marriages not because they were looking for sex, but because they craved the kind of emotional intimacy they used to have with their wives. Dr. Gray asked men specifically about what factors led them to feel emotionally dissatisfied, and the most common answer was a lack of appreciation.

When people are married for a long time, it's easy to take for granted all of the things their spouses do for them. If it's the husband's job to take out the garbage, the wife stops thanking him for doing it. If it's the wife's responsibility to drive the children around, the husband stops thanking her for it. As Dr. Gray puts it, "Somehow, we've concluded that whatever is expected of our spouse is not worthy of appreciation." Think back to the discussion on positive reinforcement. Remember the B. F. Skinner quote, "The consequences of an act occurring affect the probability of its occurring again." If nothing your spouse does results in reward, it's possible that they'll stop doing it – or they'll look for their reward elsewhere. And when I say reward, I'm not talking about sex. I'm talking about appreciation. Not just for taking out the garbage, although that's important, but appreciation for everything they do for you and everything that you love about them. Appreciation for being a great husband. Appreciation for being handsome and caring. Appreciation for going to work every day and paying the bills on time. Appreciation for buying the groceries. The best way to make sure that your marriage stays strong, healthy and faithful is to show appreciation.

Often when people stop appreciating their spouse, it is because they have gotten caught in the trap of needing reciprocation. They think, "Well, my spouse never thanks me for doing the dishes, so why should I thank him for washing the car?" As with most things in life, you have to give before you can get. You must show appreciation before you can expect it in return. Do special things for your spouse. Buy them little presents. Bake them cookies. Take them out to dinner. And always be on the lookout for things to appreciate about your spouse. Thank them for every little thing they do for you, and praise their efforts. My husband likes making breakfast for us.

Every time he does, I tell him how much I appreciate it and how delicious it is. I thank him even though I cook for the two of us more often than he does, and I comment on how wonderful it is even if it's just a plate of scrambled eggs. If your husband makes you breakfast and all you can say is, "I can't believe you burned the toast," you might never have breakfast made for you again. Something else Dr. Gray says in his book is that men start to feel as though they can't win. If they get criticized when they don't make an effort, *and* they get criticized when they do make an effort, why would they bother? When you get rewarded, you want to do a good job, and you want to do it more often.

When Dr. Gray published his book, he found that many people were offended by the notion that they could be to blame for their spouse's cheating. Cheating is not acceptable under any circumstances. However, when a relationship breaks down, rarely is it only the fault of one party. Many of the men in Dr. Gray's studies never had any intention of cheating. They wanted to have a loving and faithful marriage. But when things went wrong, and they didn't know how to fix them, they found comfort in someone else. We love people that make us feel good and make us feel special. When you stop making your spouse feel special, they will look for that feeling elsewhere. Chances are he won't actively be looking for it, but when someone new starts working in his office and that woman makes him feel like a superhero, he won't be able to resist it. You have to be the one to make your spouse feel like a superhero. If you keep someone happy they won't look elsewhere, and the easiest way to keep them happy is to appreciate them.

Caveat

The Gratitude Trap

There aren't many downsides to gratitude, but there is one. Sometimes gratitude can make you feel beholden to someone who doesn't deserve to have you around. When someone does something nice for you, you may feel obligated to keep them in your life, even when they've stopped being so nice. A good friend of mine, let's call her Amy, moved to the United States a few years ago. When she first arrived, she didn't know anyone. One of her coworkers, let's call her Betty, took her under her wing and gave her a social life. They spent all kinds of time together, and Betty smoothed Amy's transition to a new country. But when Amy had made other friends and wasn't quite so dependent on Betty, Betty wasn't too happy. She became demanding and unreasonable, and it became clear just how selfish she was. Betty continues, years later, to cause nothing but problems for my friend. But Amy can't bring herself to stop being friends with Betty because she's so grateful to her for being her friend when she first came to town. Obviously it's appropriate to feel grateful to someone who has done you a huge favor. It's even reasonable to give them more latitude than you might give to someone else. But it does not give them a license to treat you badly indefinitely. At some point you have to cut them off. The same concept applies to family members who are toxic to your mental health. You can be grateful to your parents for raising you and giving you food and shelter, and you can do everything you can to have a positive relationship with them. But if no matter what you do, they treat you badly or undermine you, you have to walk away. Don't let gratitude hold you hostage.

CONCLUSION

"Live long and prosper." – Star Trek

We have reached the end of our journey. Thank you for taking it with me. You now have the tools to make yourself the luckiest person you know. Your future is bright, sunny and filled with possibility. I hope you have already made some positive changes, and I hope you've already begun to see those positive changes pay off. Before I leave you to continue your pursuit of a lucky life, I have a few parting notes:

(1) **You will never be able to follow all of the tenets all of the time.** Or, at least, I've never been able to, so I'd be very impressed if you did. None of us are perfect. All we can do is our best. I try to be nice, but sometimes I'm not. I try to like everyone I meet, but sometimes I don't. I try not to complain, but sometimes I've just got to. Sometimes it feels as though I break my rules as often as I follow them, but I never stop trying to follow them. After all, I know they work: I am extraordinarily lucky.

Some of my good fortune can be attributed to chance alone, but most of it can't. Most of it comes from following the lucky tenets. I know this to be true because I saw how much better my life became when I learned how to be lucky. I wrote this book for those of you who, just like me, only needed a push in the right direction.

(2) **Trust your instincts.** If something doesn't feel right to you, you don't have to do it. Some things will come more naturally than others. There may be things you'll never get the hang of exactly, and other things might feel downright wrong. If you're avoiding trying something out of fear, it might be worth being brave and giving it a go anyway. But it's not necessary to follow every rule. Not everything is going to apply to you, and you don't have to abide by every tenet to see positive effects. You can pick and choose your way to some good luck.

(3) **Make your own rules.** These are the rules that work for me. I hope they'll work for you, too, but feel free to develop your own strategies. Everyone has their own ideas of what will lead to good luck. A friend of mine likes being pessimistic. She feels like it helps her to better anticipate anything that might go wrong. It's not for me, but it works for her. Another guy I know thinks that he's luckiest when he goes to bed by 9pm every night and wakes up by 5am every morning. To each their own. If you have a rule that seems incompatible

with mine, but it works for you, go with yours. Send me an email and let me in on your secret!

(4) **Believe.** Just as everything begins with belief, everything also ends with belief. Start with the belief that you can have whatever you want. Then do whatever you can to go out and get it. And then keep believing day, after day, after day.

And now all that is left is for me to wish you the best of luck.

NOTES

1. Brody, Howard. 2000. *The Placebo Response*. HarperCollins Publishers.
2. Moerman, Daniel E. 1983. "General medical effectiveness and human biology: Placebo effects in the treatment of ulcer disease." *Medical Anthropology Quarterly* 14(4):3-16.
3. Benson, Herbert and McCallie, David P., Jr. 1979. "Angina pectoris and the placebo effect." *New England Journal of Medicine* 300(25):1424-1429.
4. Moseley, J. Bruce, Jr. et al. 1996. "Arthroscopic treatment of osteoarthritis of the knee: A prospective, randomized, placebo-controlled Trial." *American Journal of Sports Medicine* 24:28-34.
5. Ariely, Dan, Ph.D. 2010. *Predictably Irrational*, Revised and Expanded Edition. Harper Perennial.
6. Rosenhan, David L. 1973. "On being sane in insane places." *Science* 179 (4070): 250-258.
7. Brafman, Ori and Brafman, Rom. 2008. *Sway*. Broadway Books.

8. Staw, Barry M. and Hoang, Ha. 1995. "Sunk costs in the NBA: Why draft order affects playing time and survival in the NBA." *Administrative Science Quarterly* 40: 474-494.
9. Schwartz, Tony. February, 9, 2003. "Relax! You'll Be More Productive." *The New York Times*.
10. Ferriss, Tim. 2009. *The 4-Hour Work Week*, Expanded and Updated Edition. Crown Publishers.
11. Levy, Becca, Slade, Martin, and Gill, Thomas. 2006. "Hearing decline predicted by elders' stereotypes." *Journal of Gerontology: Psychological Sciences* 61B(2):82-88.
12. Gilbert, D.T., Tafarodi, R.W., and Malone, P.S. 1993. "You can't not believe everything you read." *Journal of Personality and Social Psychology* 65:221-233.
13. Lowndes, Leil. 1996. *How to Make Anyone Fall in Love with You*. Contemporary Books.
14. Dijksterhuis, A. et al. 1998. "Seeing one thing and doing another: Contrast effect in automatic behavior." *Journal of Personality and Social Psychology* 75:862-871.
15. Harvey, Steve. 2009. *Act Like a Lady, Think Like a Man*. HarperCollins Publishers.
16. Chopra, Deepak. 2009. *The Ultimate Happiness Prescription*. Harmony Books.
17. Byrne, Rho nda. 2006. *The Secret*. Atria Books.
18. Giffin, Emily. 2004. *Something Borrowed*. St. Martin's Press.
19. Myers, D.G. and Diener, E. 1995. "Who is happy?" *Psychological Science* 6:10-19.
20. Brickman, P., Coates, D. and Janoff-Bulman, R. 1978. "Lottery winners and accident victims: Is happiness

relative?" *Journal of Personality and Social Psychology* 36:917-927.

21. Schlosberg, Suzanne. 2004. *The Curse of the Singles Table*. Warner Books.
22. Harrison, Jim. 1991. *Dalva*. Washington Square Press.
23. Seligman, Martin E.P. 1991. *Learned Optimism*. A.A. Knopf.
24. Wollmer, MA et al. 2012. "Facing Depression with Botulinum Toxin: A randomized controlled trial." *Journal of Psychiatric Research* 46(5):574-581.
25. Rowling, J.K. 1999. *Harry Potter and the Sorcerer's Stone*. Scholastic.
26. Lepper, M., Greene, D., and Nisbett, R.E. 1973. "Undermining children's intrinsic interest with extrinsic reward: A test of the 'overjustification' hypothesis.' *Journal of Personality and Social Psychology* 28:129-137.
27. Robbins, Anthony. 1991. *Awaken the Giant Within*. Summit Books.
28. Gunther, Max. 1977. *The Luck Factor*. Harriman House Ltd.
29. Duhigg, Charles. 2012. *The Power of Habit*. Random House.
30. Baumeister, R.F. et al. 1998. "Ego depletion: Is the active self a limited resource?" *Journal of Personality and Social Psychology* 74:1252-1265.
31. Gladwell, Malcolm. 2008. *Outliers*. Little, Brown and Company.
32. Ericsson, K.A., Krampe, R.T., and Tesch-Romer, C. 1993. "The role of deliberate practice in the acquisition of expert performance." *Psychological Review* 100(3):363-406.

33. Bond, C.F., Jr. and Titus, L.T. 1983. "Social facilitation: A meta-analysis of 241 studies." *Psychological Bulletin* 94:265-292.
34. Mlodinow, Leonard. 2008. *A Drunkard's Walk*. Vintage Books.
35. Watson, Julie and Kellner, Tomas. February 26, 2004. "J.K. Rowling and the Billion-Dollar Empire." *Forbes.com*
36. Tropper, Jonathan. 2004. *The Book of Joe*. Bantam Dell.
37. Gunther, Max. 1977. *The Luck Factor*. Harriman House Ltd.
38. Robbins, Tom. 1976. *Even Cowgirls Get the Blues*. Bantam Books.
39. Cainer, Jonathan. May 3, 2009. "Aires Daily Forecast." Cainer.com.
40. Lowndes, Leil. 1996. *How to Make Anyone Fall in Love with You*. Contemporary Books.
41. MacDonald, T.K. and Ross, M. 1999. "Assessing the accuracy of predictions about dating relationships: How and why do lovers' predictions differ from those of observers?" *Personality and Social Psychology Bulletin* 25:1417-1429.
42. Sutherland, Amy. 2008. *What Shamu Taught Me about Life, Love, and Marriage*. Random House.
43. Gilbert, Elizabeth. 2010. *Committed*. Viking.
44. Lowndes, Leil. 2001. *How to Be a People Magnet*. Contemporary Books.
45. Nowicki, S. and Duke, M.P. 1992. "The association of children's nonverbal decoding abilities with their popularity, locus of control, and academic achievement." *Journal of Genetic Psychology* 153(4):385-393.

46. Gladwell, Malcolm. 2005. *Blink*. Little, Brown and Company.
47. Bechara, A. et al. 1997. "Deciding advantageously before knowing the advantageous strategy." *Science* 275:1293-1295.
48. Chang, P.P. et al. 2002. "Anger in young men and subsequent premature cardiovascular disease: The precursors study." *Archives of Internal Medicine* 162(8):901-906.
49. Nisbett, R.E. and Wilson, T.D. 1977. "The halo effect: Evidence for the unconscious alteration of judgments." *Journal of Personality and Social Psychology* 35:250-256.
50. Gladwell, Malcolm. 2005. *Blink*. Little, Brown and Company.
51. Ambady, N. et al. 2002. "Surgeons' tone of voice: A clue to malpractice history." *Surgery* 132(1):5-9.
52. Gunther, Max. 1977. *The Luck Factor*. Harriman House Ltd.
53. Curtis, R.C. and Miller, K. 1986. "Believing another person likes or dislikes you: Behaviors making the beliefs come true." *Journal of Personality and Social Psychology* 51:284-290.
54. Lowndes, Leil. 2001. *How to Be a People Magnet*. Contemporary Books.
55. Brafman, Ori and Brafman, Rom. 2008. *Sway*. Broadway Books.
56. Kumar, N., Scheer, L, and Steenkamp, J. 1995. "The effects of supplier fairness on vulnerable resellers." *Journal of Marketing Research* 32:54-65.
57. Sutherland, Amy. 2008. *What Shamu Taught Me about Life, Love, and Marriage*. Random House.

58. Carnagie, Dale. 1936. *How to Win Friends and Influence People*. Pocket Books.
59. Wood, A.M., Froh, J.J., and Geraghty, A.W.A. 2010. "Gratitude and well-being: A review and theoretical integration." Clinical Psychology Review 30(7):890-905.
60. Emmons, Robert A. 2007. *Thanks!* Houghton Mifflin.
61. Emmons, R.A. and McCullough, M.E. 2003. "Counting blessings versus burdens: An experimental investigation of gratitude and subjective well-being in daily life." *Journal of Personality and Social Psychology* 84:377-89.
62. Emmons, Robert A. 2007. *Thanks!* Houghton Mifflin.
63. Neuman, M. Gary. 2008. *The Truth about Cheating*. John Wily & Sons, Inc.

ABOUT THE AUTHOR

All the Luck is Beth Bruder's first book. Prior to becoming a writer, Beth worked as a senior statistical analyst at a large health care company. Beth holds a Bachelor's degree in Economics from the Wharton School of Business as well as a Masters degree in Quantitative Methods for the Social Sciences from Columbia University.

Beth has been a lifelong, avid reader. She balances her love of romance novels with works from all genres, including heavy doses of social psychology and self-help. After seeing the positive influence of these books in her own life, she developed a desire to write one of her own.

When Beth isn't reading or writing, she can be found playing hockey or watching her beloved New York Rangers.

After many years of living in New York, Beth and her husband recently relocated to Toronto.

For more information, visit www.bethbruder.com or email Beth at bethbruder@bethbruder.com.